Space: 1999

Complete Series

Viewer's Guide:

Collector's Edition

BOOKS BY THE SAME AUTHOR

Non-Fiction

Blakes 7 Season One Guide

Gerry and Sylvia Anderson's UFO
Volume One Straker and Foster

Lost in Space Classic Series Guide

Sapphire & Steel Viewer's Guide

Space:1999 Year One Viewer's Guide

Space:1999 Year Two Viewer's Guide

Space:1999 Complete Series Viewer's Guide:
Collector's Edition

The Quatermass Experiment and its Legacy

The Tomorrow People: Original Series Guide

Fiction

Damon Dark: Biodome.

Lethbridge-Stewart: The New Unusual.
By Adrian Sherlock and Andy Frankham-Allen.

Space: 1999

Complete Series

Viewer's Guide:

Collector's Edition

Adrian Sherlock

2023

DEDICATED TO

Sylvia Anderson.

And those lost friends in time and space,

Martin Landau,

Barry Morse

&

Zienia Merton

SPACE: 1999

Year One

INTRODUCTION

I first saw *Space:1999* upon its television debut in Australia in the early 1970s. Australia had only just gotten colour television at that time and my household was yet to upgrade to this happy new era in television viewing, so I saw it in black and white. The design work on *Space:1999* was so good that it actually looked striking and stylish in black and white, and it also seemed very scary, too.

I was very much a child of the space age and was excited and fascinated by all the news that abounded at the time about the Apollo Moon landings. At school, I was borrowing books about the Moon missions and space exploration and reading them with great enthusiasm and like many young people, dreaming of being an astronaut.

I first encountered science fiction with *Lost in Space* and then some reruns of *Thunderbirds* and *UFO*. This notion that science fiction was dramatizing what might be possible in the future was something which really excited my imagination.

Then, just a matter of months after becoming aware of science fiction, I saw a trailer on television for a new series which was coming soon. The trailer was largely comprised of the opening title sequence of 'Breakaway'. *Space:1999* was coming soon and I was so thrilled that I ran to the kitchen table and tried to draw the Eagle spaceship I had seen. The first impression of an Eagle was amazing. There was something thrilling about the design. I don't think my drawings that day were very accurate, but it had made an impact and I could not wait for the series to begin.

I was not aware at the time, but apparently ITC and Lew Grade had chosen Australia to be a kind of test market for the series, to try out their marketing and promotional tactics.

As a youngster I was soon able to collect *Space:1999* swap cards along with most of the other boys in my neighbourhood and school. In Australia, these cards were released by the Sunicrust bread company. This meant you got one card with each loaf of bread and as a result the level of bread consumption in my home soon increased. My Nanna collected a card or two for me and was sure to give them to me, as she knew I was a fan of this show.

Naturally, my parents eventually bought me a Dinky Eagle Transporter toy, which I took to school and played with in the school yard, mainly in the sand pit where I presumably lost an atomic waste cannister or two.

Over the years, *Space:1999* became a series that I always watched whenever it was on, no matter how many times I had seen an episode before.

How does one begin to say thank you for the gift of a series that gave me so much? I guess this book is my way.

THE VOID AHEAD

In the mid-1970s, American Martin Landau became a bold, space traveling hero called Commander John Koenig in the most expensive TV series ever made, *Space:1999*.

Often misunderstood, the series is much like the Biblical story of Noah's Ark with Earth's moon adrift in the cosmos, at the mercy of time-space warps and other "stargates" inspired by *2001: A Space Odyssey*.

For Commander Koenig, his journey is one which will take him from believing his adventures are random and accidental, to a kind of faith that there are higher intelligences in the Universe and that the destiny of his people, out there in deepest space, has a meaningful purpose.

Created by Gerry and Sylvia Anderson, *Space:1999* remains one of television Science Fiction's finest examples of adventure, drama and intellectualism. While the basic premise of the series might not sound like the basis for a highly intelligent series, at first glance, the series surpasses expectations when watched in its entirety, transcending its format to become a remarkable and unforgettable viewing experience.

Lets' take a trip back in time.

It's 1973 and Man has just landed on the Moon. A new TV series goes into production in the UK, a series which will set out to capture the spirit of the time by focusing on a lunar colony in the year 1999.

The series has had a highly unorthodox beginning and will kick off with an equally unorthodox premise.

For series producer Sylvia Anderson, the task of producing the most expensive television series ever made is both a triumph in a stellar career and a tough challenge, one she will rise to with remarkable skill and grace.

Her husband at the time, Gerry Anderson, is the man behind both the premise and the casting of Martin Landau and Barbara Bain, best known at the time as the husband and wife acting team from American spy series *Mission: Impossible*.

Despite the fact these decisions are not entirely to her liking, Sylvia will turn the situation around and produce one of the most stylish and aesthetically beautiful series ever made.

Featuring state of the art visual effects and designs from experts who worked on *2001: A Space Odyssey* and costumes by American-Austrian designer Rudi Gernreich, the series will be truly spectacular. It will also be a perfect capturing of the spirit of the time, an embodiment of what Neil Armstrong's first steps on the Moon meant to the people of the world, the sense that human destiny lies out there, in deep space, among the stars and that the giant leap for Mankind into deep space had truly begun.

SYLVIA ANDERSON: THE PRODUCER OF

SPACE: 1999 YEAR ONE

This story begins in Britain, and it begins in very humble terms. A young lady by the name of Sylvia was looking for a job one day when she saw a very small job ad in the newspaper asking for someone to do secretarial work for a small film production company. Sylvia went along to the building where the film production company was based and met the people who had started the company. One of the people she would meet there was a man called Gerry Anderson.

When Gerry Anderson and Arthur Provis decided to start their own small company, A.P Films, Sylvia went along as part of the team.

The small company was not very impressive according to Gerry Anderson. They had an office and a telephone and some pencils and some notepaper with the name of their film company printed across the top of the paper and that was all.

The team had been initially involved in making the opening titles sequences for British cinema films. The one thing they were very good at was making impressive opening titles.

Sylvia ended up marrying Gerry and becoming known as Sylvia Anderson. One of the first opportunities to come to the new film production company came from a children's author named Roberta Leigh.

She had been given a small budget to make a TV series and was looking for a production company which could make the series on a low budget. Gerry Anderson has said that he was the hungriest, so he made the lowest and best offer.

When Roberta informed him that the series was to be short episodes for children and made with puppets, Gerry 's heart fell. However, Gerry and his partner Arthur, along with Sylvia, produced the series anyway and it became known as *The Adventures of Twizzle*. The same team went on to produce two more puppet series aimed at small children before Gerry decided he wanted to overcome the problems and limitations of puppet movement by introducing a futuristic vehicle into the next show.

Sylvia wrote a new storyline as a type of children's book herself, for the new series. In a way it was almost like she was demonstrating that Gerry did not need another story written by Roberta Leigh or other writers because she was capable of writing a story and creating characters just as well as Roberta had done.

This new series was called *Super Car*. *Super Car* became the first example of the type of futuristic adventure series with which Gerry and Sylvia Anderson would make their name and reputation.

Their level of artistic growth continued to rise higher and higher with each subsequent production. *Fireball XL 5* and *Stingray* both showed enormous progress, but it was *Thunderbirds* which really made the names of Gerry and Sylvia Anderson world-famous as a brand to take seriously in the entertainment business.

Thunderbirds would take the world by storm and become a lasting pop cultural legend, a series which would remain a household name thereafter.

Soon, Sylvia and Gerry realised their long-held dream of leaving puppets and children's television behind and transitioned into working with live action and real actors for the movie Doppelganger and then the much-admired classic TV series *UFO*. While dogged by poor distribution and poor programming decisions, causing both to fall short of potential success, both projects announced the Andersons as producers just as competent with live action as they were with puppets.

A proposed second season of *UFO* evolved into the seeds of *Space:1999*. Boasting an international cast of A list actors, visual effects, and production values to rival the cinematic masterpiece *2001: A Space Odyssey* and the largest budget ever raised for a television series, *Space:1999* arrived as a crowning glory to the Andersons' career.

Fate would have it that only one season of 24 episodes would be produced by Sylvia Anderson, but for one shining moment, this amazing woman whose career in television had begun in such a humble manner, was the producer of the most expensive and spectacular television series ever made.

It is to her memory and her triumph that this book is dedicated.

THIS EPISODE:

BREAKAWAY

(SPACE: 1999 PILOT EPISODE)

SCREENPLAY - GEORGE BELLAK

DIRECTED - LEE H KATZIN

It's September 13, 1999, but the caption on the screen reads 'The Dark Side of the Moon', not the far side of the Moon like one might expect. Some might think this is a problem, but the term Dark Side of the Moon is signalling, perhaps, from the very beginning that *Space:1999* is almost poetic in its intentions.

It is more about art than science. This then is almost a metaphor for shows like *Star Trek*, this is the beginning of television doing what only Stanley Kubrick had done previously in the cinema, in *2001: A Space Odyssey*, a tale which looks like it's about hard science and technology, but unfolds like poetry, full of grace notes and imagery that alludes to more that it attempts to define.

If we must look at it scientifically, then perhaps this is the side of the Moon which is currently in darkness.

The cold open of 'Breakaway' is one of the most

compelling ever broadcast. We are immediately introduced to a lunar surface where humans are at work, astronauts are on their way to check atomic leakage sensor ray readings at a nuclear waste disposal area. Meanwhile, Dr Helena Russell and Professor Victor Bergman are watching from inside a nearby enclosure. It's not clear at this point why they are watching or even who they exactly are, but Helena Russell is monitoring the brainwave activity of the astronauts.

While this plays out, an Eagle is approaching the Moon from Earth and inside it, we are introduced to the hero of the series, Commander John Koenig, played by the late, great Martin Landau. Some might argue that his status as hero of the show was usurped unintentionally and in fact effortlessly by the charming Nick Tate as astronaut Alan Carter, but there is no doubt that the great Martin Landau gives an intense and totally committed performance as the new Commander who takes over Alpha just in time to become an unintentional explorer, and student, of the Universe.

There is a lot of exposition conveyed to the viewer in our first scene with the Commander. As he talks to his boss, Commissioner Simmonds, (Roy Dotrice) we learn that Koenig is on a mission to get a space probe launched to investigate the mysterious planet Meta, which is sending out signals into space and could be harbouring life as we know it.

We learn that in orbit around the Moon is a space

station, the Centauri space dock and at the space station is the Meta probe, a giant space probe ready to set off to explore Meta. We get an early hint in this scene that Koenig is a man who harbours a passion for space exploration, a man who is dedicated to the work of astronauts and finding out what is out there. This point would come up again in the episode "Dragon's Domain", in which we find out more about Koenig's background.

Back on the Moon, Helena reacts as the instruments register that something is very wrong and one of the two astronauts on the lunar surface goes completely out of his mind. The astronaut going berserk gives the first episode of the series its most frightening moment of space-based horror, just before the opening titles crash in. Truly remarkable slow-motion photography and careful use of Kirby wires enables the crazed astronaut to fight with his fellow astronaut on the lunar surface in a convincing way, capturing the idea of the Moon's low gravity environment. The fight is dreamlike and surreal. In the early 1970s some viewers saw this in black-and-white, which made it seem even more sinister and dreamlike in quality.

Even viewed today in high definition on Blu-ray, it stands up as a highly effective and impressive sequence. As a viewer at the time, I noticed the visor one of the astronauts, the hapless Nordstrom who was going crazy, flew open momentarily during the fight, but to my mind as a child, this only added fuel to the fire, another reason why he was so insane. It never occurred to me that this was an error in production and editing. Despite this small error, the opening sequence of 'Breakaway' remains one of the series very best.

The crazy astronaut runs straight into the laser barrier which protects the nuclear waste area, deflects off it and strikes his helmet visor on a lunar boulder, cracking the glass.

As the air escapes we see in a disturbing close-up that his left eye has become horrifically changed, thanks to one of the earliest uses of a special effects contact lens. It is now mutated, green and opaque.

When Barry Gray's theme music cuts in, it is startling. The drum-roll and the bombastic fanfare are a knockout. Barry Gray was a master of creating big sounds and powerful music for the small screen. His experimentation at his home lead to some of the most impressive results ever heard on television.

In the mid-70s, it was nothing short of a revelation. In fact, many aspects of *Space: 1999* came as a revelation. Not only the opening theme but the sets, the costumes, the visual effects, the quality of the cast and the incredible atmosphere of the series were astonishing. They drew much for *2001: A Space Odyssey*, but as this had never screened on television at the time and many younger viewers had not seen it, *Space:1999* came as a considerable surprise. So good were its production standards, they remain impressive decades later.

Martin Landau himself was an actor who could bring a sense of heavy serious drama to a role, while Barbara Bain was icy, cool, and perfectly cast as a clinical lady doctor. Between the two of them, they were completely matched to the atmosphere of the series, which was both icy and very dramatic.

Everything about 'Breakaway' announces that *Space:1999* intends to be taken as serious science fiction. The opening montage, featuring the words This Episode, was not something television viewers were used to seeing at the time. The sheer pace of the editing was much more like the MTV style of editing which became known in the 1980s. The impact of the opening credits was almost mesmerising, and it is still impressive and exciting to this day.

One of the reasons 'Breakaway' stands up so well is because the series had a budget that was enormous, and the money was all on the screen. It was all spent on the cast and the impressive visuals. After the main titles, we are introduced to the set for Main Mission, the control area of Moon Base Alpha. This set is truly inspiring and fascinating and by all accounts was a true inspiration to the cast. Main Mission is a place of light, vast spaciousness, computers, control panels and pristine technology, a thing of aesthetic beauty.

We now get to know perhaps the warmest, most lovable character in the series. Professor Victor Bergman's character seems to be a homage to Nigel Kneale's Professor Quatermass (the rocket man who was in charge of BERG, the British Experimental Rocket Group) as well as being *Space: 1999*'s equivalent of *Doctor Who*, in a way. The Professor is portrayed as an old friend of the Commander, almost a father figure to him at times, but he will go on to become a kind of philosopher of the series, often interpreting events in space and time with poetic comments such as "the Gods using us for their sport, perhaps". We get another hint of *2001*'s influence with the cover story about a virus on the Moon base, too.

After his initial meeting with Professor Bergman, Koenig proceeds to his first meeting with Dr Helena Russell. This scene is important in the series as a whole because this is the moment where John Koenig meets the woman he will grow to love. The first meeting is well done, the reaction as they lock eyes for the first time is well played. She has a small smile and a slightly starry-eyed look as she sees him for the first time. However, this rather sweet moment quickly passes as they get down to the business of discussing the situation with the Meta probe astronauts being afflicted by what appears to be an outbreak of brain damage, caused by what she believes is radiation.

In a scene not too different to the type of thing, which was a mainstay of *UFO*, Dr Russell puts it upon the Commander that decision and the responsibility for what happens with the Meta probe and its crew rests entirely on the Commander's shoulders. The episode then takes us to the Medical Centre where Koenig is looking at the dying astronauts. Bathed in eerie blue light in the Medical Centre, their eyes are gone, their skin is lumpy, and they are seriously disturbing, pathetic, tragic figures.

We next meet the man who is to be the most popular character in the entire show Alan Carter played by blonde Australian Nick Tate. Alan is immediately a character that everyone can like and warm to. His priorities and his focus are always spot on. Alan's concerned about the probe, is concerned about his friends and he's shocked when he's made aware that he's been lied to.

There is also an early example of a video conference or Skype call as we would call it nowadays. Long before that sort of technology became commonplace, we see Koenig having a full conversation with his boss Commissioner Simmonds by video. Alpha's is video monitors are black and white and cathode ray tube screens which probably seems primitive nowadays but it's not unrealistic to think of Alpha being rather like a military base, with basic black and white security monitors and video screens for surveillance.

In Main Mission, the screens are showing images such as Alpha's outside buildings, people walking around in corridors, other people communicating, an Eagle waiting on the launchpad, etc. This cleverly creates a sense which adds to the illusion that Moon base Alpha is a very real place and in Koenig's confrontation with his boss over video, we see for the first time the steel inside Commander

Koenig and a little of the fire, too, as he gets angry and demands to know why the Commissioner lied to him about the state of the astronauts.

He then sets off with Bergman to investigate the nuclear waste disposal area. This leads to one of a succession of short, sharp, potent scenes that are full of tightly edited and well shot action and excitement.

One of the astronauts goes berserk from brain damage inside the observation room with Koenig and Bergman. The crazed pilot tries to use his helmet to smash open observation port window. A guard comes running in just as Koenig is flung by the crazed man and he collides with the guard. His laser clatters to the floor, Koenig grabs the laser and fires, stunning the pilot.

Bergman helps the Commander drag the pilot out of the room, with the security guard assisting, just-in-time.

The important character of Sandra also appears short time later. She is a piece of brilliant casting from Sylvia Anderson because the character of Sandra brings a vulnerability to complement the strong, cool, icy Barbara Bain, just as Alan perfectly complements Koenig by bringing a warmth, charm and optimism lacking in the serious, strong and sometimes quite sombre Commander.

Koenig races out again in an Eagle to investigate what's going on at Alpha's second nuclear waste disposal area, and we are treated to a spectacular visual of mountains glowing red with heat.

The mountains are topped with metal domes. As Koenig's eagle flies over, electrical bolts crackle into the space sky. He soon goes out of control and crash lands.

As his Eagle crashes and comes to a rest on the lunar surface, the red mountains behind him explode!

Soon Commissioner Simmonds arrives on Alpha, demanding to see the Commander. This effectively sets up the possibility that the Commissioner will be an ongoing character in the show to lock horns with the Commander over his decisions, a troublemaker, and a potential source of ongoing drama.

The Professor has discovered what's going on, now, he's realised that the nuclear waste deposited over the years in nuclear waste disposal area one is about to go critical and could explode. The whole Eagle fleet is sent out to try and remove atomic waste canisters from the underground silos, but the effort proves to be in vain.

Suddenly the nuclear waste area goes up, electrical bolts start crackling into the sky, one Eagle is hit by a deadly nuclear flash and explodes. One of the brilliant things about the design of the Eagle is the way the nosecone or head of the Eagle can be decapitated and sure enough the head of the exploding Eagle topples out of the space sky, as if a metallic insect has been decapitated in mid-flight.

A series of explosions breaks out and then the most gargantuan explosion of all rises as a false dawn over Moon base Alpha.

In one of the most incredible shots of the entire series, the lunar landscape simply falls away, leaving empty blackness, with just the Earth hanging in space.

Alan is up in space in an Eagle and sees the explosion as a blinding burst of light and through Alan we are informed that the explosion has blasted the Moon out of Earth's orbit and sent it into space. Alan's adventure begins as he decides to go after Alpha rather than hightailing it back to Earth.

Another spectacular special effects shot is delivered as the Centauri space dock goes out of control, the Meta probe ship and an Eagle ship are sent spinning away and then the Centauri dock explodes.

The aftermath of this event involves the Alphans struggling against G forces before the nuclear waste stops fissioning and the Moon is simply adrift in space. We see a magnificent shot apparently relayed from a satellite (which is repeated endlessly at the end of the opening credits sequence for each episode) of the Moon drifting away from us and as it passes the camera, a message is broadcast from a newsreader who tells us about the impact the

Moon's sudden departure has had back on Earth, with earthquakes and other problems.

This is a clever way of conveying information to the audience about Earth's plight and the computer on Alpha totally rejects the request for a decision about evacuating the base, lumping it all back on Koenig's shoulders, once again, with the statement 'human decision required'.

This could almost be a mission statement for the character of the Commander and for the series as a whole and once again it echoes the position of the previous Commander portrayed on *UFO* by Ed Bishop. Once again the Commander has to make a human decision when faced with the outrageous and terrible situation.

The decision is that the Alphans should stay right where they are and try to adjust to the situation and survive as best they can, rather than making a desperate, dangerous, foolhardy, and possibly suicidal attempt to return to Earth. This is a key moment and Martin Landau brings the right level of sobre, regretful but dignified strength to the scene.

The base soon starts to receive signals from the planet Meta and Koenig wonders if that's where their future lies.

'Breakaway' is one of the best television pilot episodes ever produced and everything about it looks fantastic. Truly, it is slick, it is polished, it is beautiful, it is spectacular. Throughout there is an atmosphere that is almost unbearably cold, clinical, and icy and at the same time heavy, dramatic, and tense.

There is a sense of serious, adult oriented science fiction too. Many watching at the time were unable to wrap their heads around the fact that the Moon had been blasted out of orbit by nuclear explosion and what kind of situation this could mean for the rest of the series.

However, those of those of us who watched it through the eyes of childhood or simply a more open mind were prepared to accept that there could be more to the situation than just a simple case of a big enough explosion to knock the moon out of orbit.

This point is something the series would develop in surprising and intriguing ways but for now it is sufficient to say that Moon base Alpha was on its way into deep space, and it would be, in its way, the greatest probe into space ever known.

The odyssey for the 311 men and women on Moon base Alpha had begun and as actor Nick Tate said, it was going to be a bumpy ride.

COMPUTER'S OBJECTIVE ASSESSMENT

PRODUCTION QUALITY

10/10

Despite a few minor bloopers the overall production quality is outstanding.

It looks like a movie of similar quality to *2001: A Space Odyssey* has come to television, at least at face value with loads of Eagle action and explosions galore.

Although it's a little slow and stilted in some of the early scenes, 'Breakaway' remains one of the most spectacular television pilot episodes ever produced.

Our very vulnerable human heroes are hurled into the unknown in spectacular and powerful fashion.

The show was off to a brilliant start.

THIS EPISODE:

MATTER OF LIFE AND DEATH

SCREENPLAY - ART WALLACE AND JOHNNY BYRNE

DIRECTED - CHARLES CRICHTON

Johnny Byrne was a master of the ghost story and when he rewrote Art Wallace's script for 'Matter of Life and Death', he turned this tale of Helena's reunion with her husband Lee, lost in space and presumed dead, into a science fiction ghost story with many eerie and intriguing moments.

Wallace had contributed scripts to the original *Star Trek* series including a memorable story called 'Obsession' and here he wanted to tell the tale of a kind of trap which would use the image of a loved one, such as Helena's missing husband Lee, as bait to lure victims to their doom in the manner of the Sirens of ancient mythology.

However, Wallace apparently wrote the script before the format for *Space:1999* was given its final shape and form by George Bellak. Bellak had moved *Space:1999*'s format much closer to a blatant television version, albeit unofficially, of *2001: A Space Odyssey*. There would have been other changes, such as Alpha being given its name after initially being called Moon City and even

Wander. The character names and roles of the regulars may also have changed between Wallace writing and the time when Byrne was tasked with a rewrite.

In writing the final version, Byrne made a lot of changes to the premise of the episode. No longer a trap involving fake loved ones as bait, planet Terra Nova is now something much more mysterious and enigmatic and Lee Russell seems genuine, if changed on a fundamental level.

Often seen as the second episode of the series, possibly because 'Black Sun' was still in post-production, it feels like the cast are still feeling their way at times.

Barbara Bain is very restrained considering the emotional potential of the plot. Her husband Lee has been missing for a long time, presumed dead in deep space. When Lee reappears aboard an Eagle on its way back to Moon base Helena is reunited with him. This is where the episode perhaps misses its greatest opportunity for dramatic impact.

The revelation of the mystery man aboard the Eagle, and Helena's line that it's her husband, is the perfect place at which to hear the drum roll and cut to the opening titles sequence of the episode.

Possibly a lingering close up of Koenig's astonished reaction might have been a great way to show how this twist impacts him. But the episode pulls its punch here and the moment comes off much flatter than it should.

The opening titles arrive earlier, before the Eagle even lands, the opening hook ending with the much less dramatic moment of Koenig announcing a yellow alert.

However, this is a minor criticism, and the episode picks up interest as it goes along.

In the Medical Centre on the Moon base, Lee eventually awakens and says Helena called him. Helena does not ever give us any indication that she called him in any real sense. Presumably Helena called him only on a subconscious and mental level. Somehow the missing husband has latched onto her subconscious thoughts and feelings on a psychic level.

In another scene Helena touches her face and hand with her wedding ring as we see Lee lying in the hospital bed. It is as if there is an unspoken almost psychic connection between them in this scene.

The Professor also tells the Commander that there is an indication that Lee is drawing strength and energy from Helena. Heat scans of the body show that when Helena is not present Lee's body appears to be cold and dead. "Matter of Life and Death" is therefore a ghost story, at least in essence.

The ghost of Helena's husband has returned to her, but they can never be together because he is now opposite to her and us humans. As the episode progresses Lee attempts to warn the Alphans not to visit the planet Terra Nova. When he realises they do not believe him and will not listen to him he appears to die but his body soon vanishes.

When the humans go down to the planet they find a paradise. But the paradise sours and turns into a hostile nightmare and everyone seems to die except for Helena. Even the Moon itself seems to explode. Then Lee simply reappears, and everything is restored to normal. This type of resolution is what would now be called a reset, but it is unclear if the events on Terra Nova were real or an illusion of sorts.

Although Helena and Professor Bergman assume that Lee is anti-matter, his only response to the suggestion is "if you like", not a definitive "yes". What is obvious is that humans have been shown danger, so they can understand the fact that they cannot stay on the planet.

Everyone leaves Terra Nova, returning to Alpha and the episode ends with Helena staring out the window at the planet is the moon drifts away. Koenig sees the sad wistful look on her face. Her husband is out there but he is no longer like us and they can never be together. It's all rather sad and haunting.

Byrne apparently would have preferred to abandon Wallace's script and write a fresh story instead and he apparently disliked the type of ending in which everyone dies and then are seen to be alive again, as in a dream episode or reset-button resolution. But despite his reservations, he manages to deliver a potent, if somewhat ambiguous plot, which encapsulates his love of the sad ghost story, and it is both unnerving and touching at times.

Although the episode has its weaknesses such as very understated acting from Barbara Bain in what should've been her most emotional episode it is nevertheless haunting science-fiction rendition of a ghost story about loss and the sorrow of a loving couple who can never be together.

'Matter' should probably not be the second episode of the series. It was probably written with an idea in mind of it being seen a little later in the series, after the Moon had made more progress across space, but it still sort of works in production order.

Johnny Byrne had a great gift for writing ghost stories, and this would appear again and again in the series, culminating in 'The Troubled Spirit'.

COMPUTER'S OBJECTIVE ASSESSMENT

OVERALL PRODUCTION QUALITY

8/10

A little slow, but very competent and featuring a spectacular storm sequence on the planet Terra Nova in the finale. The planet set is awesome, and the exploding Moon is startling.

The plot is a little muddled and the explanations are ambiguous and frustrating for the casual viewer.

At times, some of the acting is still a little stilted, too, but the episode delivers plenty of intrigue, spooky atmosphere, and chills.

A sad, touching ending helps make it worthy for the true fan.

THIS EPISODE:

THE BLACK SUN

SCREENPLAY - DAVID WEIR

DIRECTED - LEE H KATZIN

The 'Black Sun' is one of the most significant and popular episodes of the entire series. It's not perfect and there is a minority opinion that it's not very interesting and in fact rather boring, but certainly among *Space:1999* fans, it is a firm favourite and has great significance for the series as a whole.

People often think of 'Black Sun' as an ensemble episode; however it is very much an hour which belongs to Barry Morse, it is Professor Bergman's big episode. Morse is brighter here than anywhere else and first season fans, especially those who cannot stomach the second season because of the fact Barry Morse is not in it, tend to hold this episode in very high regard.

Certainly, Morse shines as Bergman in this episode with some wonderful dialogue and many fine moments in which he cements the idea that the Professor has an almost father and son relationship with John Koenig. If anything negative is to be said about this one, it's that it does seem to take Bergman a long time to work out that the big, round black thing out in space is a black hole.

However, since *Space:1999* was the first television series to dramatize the existence of black holes in 1973, we can forgive the writer for presenting it this way.

The episode gets off to a lively start with plenty of interesting incident involving an asteroid which plunges toward Alpha, only to veer off into space and mysteriously disintegrate. There is a guest appearance by the lead singer of Manfred Mann, Paul Jones, too. He plays Sandra's boyfriend Mike, and the episode generates considerable drama as Mike is sent to investigate the titular 'Black Sun', as the Professor argues with the computer and potters around in his lab, trying to work out some calculations and figure out what is going on. Of course, Bergman works it out faster than the computer, but just not fast enough to save Mike from destruction.

Mike's death is a highlight of the episode and Director Lee H Katzin uses some of the special effects lens techniques he had employed previously on shows like *Mission Impossible.* The sense of time and space distorting as Mike's Eagle ship is sucked into the 'Black Sun' before it explodes is really well done thanks to the bizarre lens effect and was mesmerising at the time it was first shown.

The death of Mike has a big impact on Sandra, who faints, with Paul rushing to tend to her. But it is Professor Bergman who dominates the proceedings as Alpha heads towards the 'Black Sun'. There are strong doses of Alfred Hitchcock's film *Lifeboat* as Koenig gets the computer to do the equivalent of drawing straws to decide which Alphans will go on an Eagle survival ship, while everyone else remains on Alpha to face the danger of the 'Black Sun'.

Martin Landau and Barbara Bain are both very good here, conveying their strong if understated feelings for each other as Koenig insists Helena go off into space in the survival ship, and other characters get good moments as well, but this is very much Barry Morse's episode.

As the Moon nears the 'Black Sun', Alpha protected somewhat by his force-field, the old Professor comes alive as he philosophises and faces death with not only dignity but childlike fascination. Morse apparently strongly argued against his character wearing the standard Moon base Alpha uniform as he felt it was not the type of thing a professor like Victor Bergman would wear.

Morse wanted to give Professor Bergman characterisation and personality and it is in this episode that he comes closest to being allowed to realise his ideas for Bergman's personality on screen.

As the moon hurtles towards apparent doom, Bergman breaks out the cigars and some 50-year-old Brandy he's been saving for a special occasion in an old bag, as well as a rather colourful scarf.

In one of the most loved and quoted moments of

the series, Bergman and Koenig drink a toast, with Koenig saying, "to everything that might have been" and Bergman responding, "to everything that was!"

It is a very fine moment which really resonates with fans of the series and has only become more poignant with the passage of time.

If I had to point out a flaw in this episode it would be the fact that it lacks a strong sense of complex narrative or a troublemaking antagonist and therefore has much less appeal than usual to non-fans and casual viewers, some of whom complain that the episode is simply overblown and tedious, calling it a talkfest.

However, if you are charmed by the warmth of Barry Morse as Bergman, you will adore this episode. 'Black Sun' also does something very good for the series in that the drifting moon is drawn into a black hole which turns out to be the gateway to a kind of space-time wormhole, then emerges through what appears to be a white hole on the other side of the Universe, a million light-years away. With the moon now transported into a totally different region of space, it becomes far more plausible the Earth people can then encounter other star systems and other planets.

The episode also attempts to at least suggest that there was an alien interference in the event which blew the Moon out of earth orbit, the 'Breakaway'.

The journey through the 'Black Sun' happens with

the support, assistance or perhaps guidance of some kind of unseen godlike alien intelligence which talks to the Commander and the Professor during a rather surreal sequence in which they first become like ghosts and then become incredibly old.

The voice of this mysterious entity is female, and it should be apparent that the writer of the episode and the story editor were having a lot of fun turning the notion of God being male on its head. This episode, more than any other, sets up the idea that Alpha's journey has more to it than meets the eye, that there is not just a random nuclear accident casting moon out of Earth orbit, but that the moon is on an odyssey instigated and perhaps guided with purpose by an enigmatic intelligence.

It suggests that its journey through space, which on the face of it may seem to defy conventional laws of physics, is due to other things, such as intervention of an alien intelligence and its powers, which may be beyond comprehension.

The episode is the first, but not the last, to indicate that the Moon is passing through space time wormholes and other portals, which enable it to move much further out into the universe than would have been possible from just a nuclear explosion.

These implications are not explored or written in a great deal of detail, however. Instead, they are left commendably enigmatic and mysterious, leaving us to wonder, leaving the characters to wonder as well.

Someone or something helped Alpha survive the 'Breakaway' and now it has helped them pass through the 'Black Sun' and they are far across the Universe in unknown space.

The odyssey is one in which the journey and the destination of the Moon and its inhabitants is still unknown.

So, was the 'Black Sun' itself an equivalent to the star-gate from *2001: A Space Odyssey*? One of the fundamental differences between film and television is that television requires a group of characters to act as an ensemble who can talk to each other and convey stories through dialogue whereas a movie can focus on one character by himself.

Just as the movie *The Time Machine* focuses on one time traveller in his time machine, the TV equivalent, *Doctor Who*, requires a larger time machine which can contain three or four time-travellers so that it can have an ensemble of characters to carry the series.

We see this again when we compare *Space: 1999* to the movie which obviously inspired it, Stanley Kubrick's *2001: A Space Odyssey*. A pod containing one man, Dave Bowman, passes through a Star Gate and is transported to another part of the universe in the finale of *2001*, but in the 'Black Sun', the whole moon and Moon base containing a huge crew, an ensemble of characters, passes through the 'Black Sun' which acts as a kind of Star

Gate, transporting the ensemble to the other side of the universe.

The 'Black Sun' was directed by the same director who worked on 'Breakaway', Lee H Katzin, and was obviously intended as the second half of the introduction story for the series. 'Breakaway' and 'Black Sun' together are kind of TV equivalent to *2001*, sending the ensemble to the distant regions of the universe where further episodes of their odyssey can play out.

Katzin obviously wanted to hint at the poetic soul of the series, too, because just as 'Breakaway' opens with a caption that feels inspired by Pink Floyd's *Dark Side of the Moon*, the 'Black Sun' ends with a line from Bergman which feels inspired by a Beatles song, *Across the Universe*.

COMPUTER'S OBJECTIVE ASSESSMENT

OVERALL PRODUCTION QUALITY

10/10

While some viewers may find it a little slow and talkative, the attention to production detail is outstanding, with superb camera work and impressive visuals for the 'Black Sun' itself.

The acting is of a very high calibre and there is much humanity on display as the Alphans face doom with dignity.

The plot resolution may confound some casual viewers, but this is top shelf all the same and an essential episode for any true fan, particularly those who love Barry Morse as Bergman.

Through this experience, Koenig begins to find his faith that someone is watching over Alpha in space, making it a very important episode.

THIS EPISODE:

RING AROUND THE MOON

SCREENPLAY - EDWARD DI LORENZO

DIRECTED - RAY AUSTIN

'Ring Around the Moon' is generally an episode which gets a lot less love than many others in the series and is easy to dismiss. However, it's actually a pretty good episode with some nice moments and a lot to enjoy, if one is open to delving a little deeper into it. The cold opening of the episode is particularly good because it sets up the whole situation of the episode very quickly and dramatically and with a great deal of detail.

One memorable aspect of the episode is the minor guest role of Ted Clifford who is played by Max Faulkner, a stunt man who worked repeatedly on 1970s *Doctor Who* and gradually became something of a proper actor, getting a reasonably sized role in the Tom Baker *Doctor Who* serial 'Invasion of Time'. As was often the case, Faulkner's main job here was to have a death scene, but in this case, he also gets to be rather violent and deranged as well, as the alien probe attempts to take control of him. Ted Clifford is taken over and becomes a threat to Alpha before dying unexpectedly.

A criticism levelled at this story is that instead of

calling security at once, Sandra, Paul, Kano, Koenig, and Helena all try to deal with Clifford's violent craziness themselves. Possibly this is where we need to remember the Alphans are out in deep space by accident, totally unprepared, and this may in fact be the first case of an unruly, violent, and out of control staff member in Main Mission they've ever had to deal with.

The music in the episode is very distinctive and unusual too, being scored for the episode, but not by the show's main composer Barry Gray. Instead, we get a very eclectic score which imparts a rather odd flavour. Sylvia Anderson's son-in-law Vic Elms did the music for this episode. He apparently had some trouble getting along with the other musicians involved in scoring the series, so this episode was to be the only one featuring his music cues. While very different to Gray, it's rather good fun in its way. Elms reputedly contributed the electric guitar riff in the opening theme music, too, for which fans should be eternally grateful.

The episode begins quickly enough. An eye in the sky appears in space above the Moon. A large, yellow eye with brain-like elements around it. The Cyclops eye of the Odyssey is invoked in the form of an alien space probe. It snares Alpha in an energy field and tries to take control, declaring the Earthlings its prisoner with a creepy, whispering voice.

Apparently, Prentis Hancock provided the whispering voice of the alien probe. He does a great job as it really does not sound like him and is very hard to recognise if you don't know who is speaking.

One of the big questions about 'Ring Around the Moon' is to do with the way Victor Bergman goes about deducing the backstory of the planet Triton and works out the fact that it has been destroyed in a stellar explosion long ago.

The two main pieces of evidence which lead Victor to this happy conclusion seems to be the fact that Helena returns from the probe and tells him and John that the aliens refer to themselves as the Eyes of Triton and the fact that the Egyptians appear to have noted them as the Eyes of Heaven and mapped the position of their planet.

This seems to be a reference to *ancient astronauts* and the type of thing that went on in the book "Chariots of the Gods". The *ancient astronauts* theme was a popular and common trope in 70s British science fiction. Other notable examples are *Doctor Who*'s 'Pyramids of Mars' and *The Tomorrow People*'s 'Worlds Away', which both suggest aliens were involved with ancient Egyptians and had a hand in the building of the pyramids.

The Eyes of Triton apparently came to Earth and landed in ancient Egypt and were known as the Eyes of Heaven and this is recorded in the Pyramid text of the Old Kingdom. Bergman makes the comment "it seems our friends get about a bit."

Professor Bergman finds the position of the mythical planet Triton, the home of the Eyes of Heaven, is able to match it to his star charts and astronomical information from the computer, and he sees a supernova there, the remains of an exploded star, and realises that Triton is dead, and the Triton people are now extinct.

It's this knowledge about the destruction of Triton which Koenig uses to convince the alien probe to destroy itself in the finale. The probe abducts Helena and turns her into its zombie-like slave to gather information from Alpha. This gives the episode an emotional subtext, too, as Koenig is forced to fight to save her, the woman he is clearly beginning to care deeply about, from ending up as dead as Ted Clifford.

The best thing about all this is not just that Barry Morse is typically excellent but that the Professor Bergman character, a man of science who has devoted his life to the pursuit of knowledge, realises that, despite all the knowledge that they had accumulated, the people Triton became extinct, and their world burnt up. All that knowledge was useless to them in the end. It was all for nothing.

He is left to ponder the notion that maybe knowledge isn't the answer after all, as he presumably believed it to be for most of his adult life. The ever-thoughtful Koenig helpfully poses the question, "what is?"

Perhaps this would carry even more weight

thematically had the writers sent Bergman up to the Triton probe with Koenig to confront the alien intelligence and learn a little more and experience something for himself of the Tritonians, maybe asking them a few questions, but as it stands, it is still a fascinating notion for Professor Bergman to confront.

Another understated but interesting element is when Carter learns that Donovan, his co-pilot, has died in their Eagle crash. Morrow was unable to use remote control, but when Koenig says *you were at the controls,* Carter replies he was in *Never Never Land.* (The Never Never is a remote area in Outback Australia)

Its name comes from this poem:

Out on the wastes of the Never Never -

That's where the dead men lie!

There where the heatwaves dance forever

-That's where the dead men lie!

The implication seems to be that Donovan woke up and managed to save Carter's life but died in the crash himself. This seems to motivate Carter to want to go back, changing places with Parkes.

Some other fun aspects of this episode include Alan Carter's Eagle doing a very cool spin out in space, as it hurtles back towards the Moon and then crash-lands on the lunar soil, a rather groovy slow motion Moonwalk as the Alphans don space suits to go to Alan's aid and the floating effect of Helena seemingly levitating as she is drawn towards the alien probe before vanishing in a flash, which hurls Koenig backwards onto the Moon's surface.

These moments are well handled and enjoyable in terms of visual style. The music for the bouncy Moon-walk sequence is quite rich and memorable, too.

All in all, 'Ring Around the Moon' may not be one of the best episodes, but it has more going for it than its reputation might suggest and can be enjoyed if one is prepared to look for its good points.

COMPUTER'S OBJECTIVE ASSESSMENT

OVERALL PRODUCTION QUALITY

7/10

The episode contains a number of good sequences, some of which are neat and fun to watch, but also contains some weakly imagined and cheap-looking visual effects, particularly when an Eagle splits a beam of orange light coming out of the alien sphere.

There are no guest stars apart from the brief appearance of relatively unknown actor Max Faulkner and the plot is not always clearly explained.

It's an enjoyable episode for the true fan who may be prepared to make some allowances and read between the lines for meaning, but nonfans may find it a little B grade and unimpressive.

THIS EPISODE:

EARTHBOUND

SCREENPLAY - ANTHONY TERPILOFF

DIRECTED - CHARLES CRICHTON

'Earthbound' was probably made with the intention of being retrospectively slotted in between 'Breakaway' and the 'Black Sun', as a way of wrapping up the presence of Commissioner Simmonds on Alpha. The episode begins with a discussion in a conference on Alpha about the Alphans coming to terms with their new life, trapped on Alpha and adrift in deep space.

Commissioner Simmonds makes his presence felt immediately as the antagonist of the show and in a way it's almost a pity he couldn't have been slotted into several more episodes as an antagonist and troublemaker because, firstly, might've livened up the show with his presence and, secondly, if his demise in this episode had come as a surprise to the audience after they've gotten used to him as the regular troublemaker on the show, it probably would have had an even bigger impact than it has by itself.

In many territories, this episode was not shown second and certainly on DVD and Blu-ray sets it is often fifth as in the production order, but in the test territory of Australia, 'Earthbound' was always screened as episode two. It probably seems more natural coming directly after 'Breakaway' since there would be no mystery as to where Simmonds has been during the episodes in between.

Simmonds tells Koenig that the impossible, getting back to Earth, takes just a little longer but his antics are interrupted by a message about an unidentified powered object approaching Alpha. Now, this is almost a flip side to the standard *UFO* storyline where SHADO's Moonbase would detect an unidentified flying object approaching the base, which would invariably contain aliens from a dying planet who were desperate and ruthless.

In this case, aliens from a dying planet are approaching in the unidentified powered object but instead of being ruthless killers, they come in peace. Since *Space: 1999* grew out of *UFO*, it is nice to see *UFO*'s alien premise inverted here. The ever-heroic Alan Carter is quickly dispatched into space to investigate the approaching alien craft, but the alien ship crash lands on the Moon. Koenig snaps some orders and Alan picks up the Commander, the doctor and the Professor and whisks them out to the alien ship's crash site.

The early scenes with the Alphans entering the alien craft are quite eerie and atmospheric as they find, inside the ethereal and strange interior, a series of glass coffin-like suspended animation chambers. Each has a dormant alien within. These aliens are tall, wearing long robes and have long hair. They also have face-paint which calls to mind the look of American Indians in warpaint.

The main guest actor Christopher Lee plays the alien space captain, Zantor, as very much the noble Indian, wise, even-tempered, and sombre.

But before he has awoken from his cryogenic sleep, we get another moment of *Space: 1999* horror which chilled the blood of many young viewers watching in the 1970s. Dr Russell attempts to drill a hole into one of the cryogenic chambers, but as soon as her drill begins to break the seal, a red glow lights up the interior of the transparent chamber. Then there is a flash, an explosion inside, and the whole chamber fills with smoke.

When the smoke clears, Dr Russell and the Commander see to their horror that the alien sleeping in the chamber has been reduced to a heap of black ashes.

Fortunately, when the rest of the aliens wake up they turn out to be both peaceful and forgiving about this tragic error of judgement. However, Commissioner Simmonds is not so compassionate. He wants the Commander to hijack the alien ship and use it to get six Alphans back to Earth. When the Commander refuses to go along with this Simmonds decides to take matters into his own hands. The writer of the episode cleverly wrong foots the audience with a scene in which Dr Russell tries the alien cryogenic sleep chamber and cannot seem to wake up. In one of the most gripping scenes of *Space: 1999,* Simmonds, the Commissioner, takes the Commanders com-lock device and a laser pistol and takes control of Alpha's power station.

In a disturbing scene, he plunges the whole Moonbase into darkness, threatening to leave the Alphans to freeze to death in the icy cold vacuum of space without the nuclear power they need to heat the base so they can survive. Alan Carter once again speaks in a way that is very relatable for the audience's point of view and continues to win more fans as he expresses his keenness to trick the Commissioner and take him on his way out to the ship.

Noble alien Captain Zantor does what noble aliens do. He offers to be a hostage if it will get the Commissioner off Alpha. There is almost a sense of watching the story of U.S President Richard Nixon in the character of Simmonds. Roy Dotrice delivers a blistering hatchet job on politicians everywhere as he says *I got to be Commissioner by doing what was necessary not what was right,* and like Nixon, his Watergate is inevitable.

It comes when Simmonds wakes up inside the alien ship only to discover that the cryogenic suspension has not worked on him. At this point in the narrative it should be obvious that the writer had worked on Alfred Hitchcock's anthology TV series. He understood Hitchcock-style suspense and brutal twist endings and he brings it to *Space:1999* with this ending.

Commissioner Simmonds has bought himself nothing more than a premature burial in outer space. He is alive yet trapped inside a glass coffin with no air and no way out. In one of the most shocking moments of genuine human horror ever broadcast, Simmonds realises he is trapped and goes absolutely berserk, like a wild animal, thrashing around, pounding on the glass walls and roof of the box he is in, screaming for help, before collapsing in despair.

In the ultimate irony, we learn the Alpha's computer has selected Simmonds is the most expendable member of Alpha and the right one to send back to Earth with the aliens. Had Simmonds not hijacked the spot in the alien ship by force, he probably would have survived.

The episode contains a few errors of editing, such as when Alan's co-pilot seems to vanish shortly after launch and when frozen Kaldorians seem to wake up in the background of shots near the end. Of course, such bloopers are typical of a show with a tight production schedule, things are left in, and people only notice because we can re-watch endlessly these days.

The moon base computer seems to take a long time to make its unbiased choice of which Alphan is to get a free ride back to Earth with the aliens in their ship. I assume the reason the computer takes so long is because the decision is based on whom Alpha could function without. It was presumably cross matching skills and roles, deciding who was too irreplaceable to let go.

It chose Simmonds because he was right when he said, "I have no place here on Alpha". He was useless. Koenig told Simmonds, "I need a doctor and scientist out there, not a politician." This idea of the computer choosing people based on skills or the lack thereof in Simmonds' case seems to be a consistent notion across the series. For example, in 'Black Sun', Koenig explains that the computer is choosing the people to go in the survival ship based on who is best suited to ensure the survival of Mankind in space. Again, skills and abilities are checked and cross checked before computer settles on Alan as the Captain and the others who go with him.

Later, in the series' final episode, when the Alpha crew member Anna Davis turns out to be a language expert in the episode Testament of Arcadia, which is just what the team need to decipher Sanskrit writings, Koenig remarks "perhaps computer knew something we didn't." It's a part of the series, apparently, that the computer selects the right people for things, based on who they are and what they do. Simmonds is a politician, it's totally logical the computer chose him as the one to go, the one they do not need on the base.

People being chosen for their abilities is even continued in the second season such as when Koenig thinks it strange that all three members of the radiation monitoring team would be selected to return to Earth in "Bringers of Wonder", a situation which is manipulated by the titular aliens.

As with the people who work in a Human Resources department, the Alpha computer must match people's profiles, skills, experience, roles, etc to any decision it's asked to decide upon. And it's only when faced with situations outside the limits of its data that computer declares "Human Decision Required".

'Earthbound' is a haunting episode. While at times its pace is slow and ponderous, its moments of horror are outstanding and both of the main guest stars make it memorable and high quality. Unsurprisingly, it remains one of *Space:1999*'s most well-loved episodes.

COMPUTER'S OBJECTIVE ASSESSMENT

OVERALL PRODUCTION QUALITY

10/10

The guest cast are exceptional, and the script is first rate, too. The direction is also top-notch and aims for quality.

Although the story has a slow patch in the middle and minor bloopers appear (extras playing aliens react to Simmonds and strings can be seen on the Kaldorian ship model at times) the ending is extraordinary television.

Commissioner Simmonds unravels in a spectacular example of human drama at its finest. Like Jack Torrance in *The Shining*, Simmonds descends into darkness, becoming a threat to Alpha and finally causes his own self destruction.

Christopher Lee's iconic presence also lends the episode added credibility as a true classic. A must-see episode.

THIS EPISODE:

ANOTHER TIME, ANOTHER PLACE

SCREENPLAY - JOHNNY BYRNE

DIRECTED - DAVID TOMBLIN

'Another Time, Another Place' is one of the most elaborately made and significant episodes of the entire *Space: 1999* series. It begins with a spectacular sequence in which the Moon enters an unknown phenomenon in deep space which is almost certainly a time-warp and gets sent hurtling at incredible speed into a completely different region of the Universe.

Along the way, something very strange happens. The people of Moon base and the moon itself seem to split off into two separate selves, two different timelines perhaps. Only one person, a young Alphan woman named Regina, seems to be caught mid-way in the event. She screams in horror and Helena turns to see what she is looking at. Another moon is now heading away from them!

Eerie use of dark lighting and psychedelic lighting effects in the view port windows of Main Mission, slow motion, and double exposures to show ghostly twin images of each main character, all makes the sequence come to life vividly on screen.

It's yet another brilliant cold open which hooks the audience with striking visuals and avantgarde film making. This sequence does something very good for the series, too, in that it makes a very clear and definite indication that the moon is shifting in space over a vast distance of many light years in a matter of seconds, due to the phenomenon which appears to be a space-time warp.

In practical terms it would make more logical sense for this episode to occur before 'Black Sun', even though 'Black Sun' was written and produced earlier, because the space-time warp could be anywhere in space, whereas the Black Sun would probably be a considerable distance from Earth's solar system.

This was probably writer Johnny Byrne's way of explaining Alpha's vast distance from Earth, as well as a means to introduce his imaginative ideas for the episode.

The jump across space and time which occurs in this episode means that, along with 'Black Sun', there are two examples of the moon being shifted vast distances across interstellar space in just the first half a dozen produced episodes, which explains how the Moon has managed to get so far into deep space, after the 'Breakaway', despite drifting at sub-light speed.

As was often the case, writer Johnny Byrne was more adept than most other writers on the series when it came to handling the science-fiction aspects of the series and he did a lot to make the show's over all format more believable.

One could even say Byrne all but completely rescues the runaway Moon format of the show by introducing space-time warps and a number of Alpha-based bottle episodes into the series, steering clear of potential pitfalls.

There is a third suggestion that the Moon has passed through a time-warp, a little later in the series, in the episode 'Death's Other Dominion', as well, but it is not clear when this one took place.

The fact that there are three shifts through space and time for the moon in season one, that we know about, means it is not unreasonable for Alpha to encounter the planets which it encounters. After all, only about half of the 24 episodes of the series involve Moonbase Alpha encountering planets. The other half are set on the moon as it drifts through space, being visited by spacecraft and other object.

This means on average Alpha only encounters three or four planets for each of the three times it is shifted many light-years across space by some sort of space time phenomenon. If we assume that two or three of the planets which the Alphans investigate are in the same star system as each other, then it becomes even easier to believe their travels are somewhat plausible, if only loosely explained.

This episode features Alpha emerging from the

time warp only to find it is approaching what appears to be the planet Earth. However, in a truly startling twist, it turns out that this is some form of alternative Earth, on which life no longer exists.

The humans soon discover the other moon which separated from them as they went through the space-time warp, too.

Some extremely eerie images follow as John and Alan explore a deserted, airless, crumbling Moon Base Alpha on the other moon and look inside a crashed Eagle where they discover their own dead bodies seated at the controls.

A subplot about young Regina (Judy Geeson) also proves to be horrifying as she has nightmares in which sees chilling images of her other self in a mirror when she awakens in the silent darkness of the Medical Centre and then sees her other self's face replaced by that of a dead skull.

Regina's meltdown in Main Mission, armed with a laser, is reminiscent of Shakespeare's play *Hamlet* and the scene in which poor Ophelia is out of her mind in front of the people of the castle. Judy Geeson is terrific in this sequence, delivering a committed and powerful performance.

Regina dies and one of the interesting aspects is that in her other life, Regina 's other self was apparently married to Alan.

Once again, Alan is just the perfect character for

the audience to love as he responds to Regina with gentleness and compassion, carrying her away after she collapses.

Unfortunately, someone on the production team insisted that Bergman be given the line "two brains ", as he studies a plate of Regina 's brain. This is something which writer Johnny Byrne was very happy with apparently, but I suppose we can generously excuse it as Victor Bergman speaking metaphorically, not literally. Perhaps he is thinking out loud about the idea that she was able to connect psychically with the brain of her other self, in her other life.

Everything starts to make more sense in the latter half of the episode as the Alphans go down to visit and explore the other Earth and meet up with their alternative selves. There are some truly unnerving scenes as the Alphans first encounter their twins, who have left the other moon and colonised this deserted alternative Earth.

The relationship between Paul and Sandra is seen as having reached its fulfillment here with the couple having young children. Barry Morse is terrific here as Bergman chats with Koenig and fills him in on what happened.

There is also an extremely touching and haunting scene for Barbara Bain as Helena. She meets an older version of herself who married John Koenig only to have him die on the moon surface. The widow Helena sees John Koenig and their encounter is a truly emotional moment, very well handled.

All in all this a haunting and memorable episode with many striking scenes, great visuals, and spooky moments along the way. It tells us much about the emotional undercurrents of love and connection between characters such as John and Helena and Paul and Sandra.

It also tells us much about characters like Alan Carter and even Kano gets a few good moments.

At the end of the episode, the two moons seem to collide in space and the flow of time, somehow split into two timelines by the first encounter with the space-time warp, apparently rights itself.

Things are left very ambiguous about where the Alphans had been and how this alternative group of selves came about, but the episode ends with the moon emerging from the space-time phenomena into a completely new region of the Universe, with Sandra saying, "we are in different space". The moon is now far away from Earth and ready to encounter a new star system and a new group of fascinating planets in the episodes ahead.

COMPUTER'S OBJECTIVE ASSESSMENT

OVERALL PRODUCTION QUALITY

10/10

Although the plot is little wild in places and possibly illogical, the imagery and the human horror of the story.

The episode is visually stunning and there are many touching emotional scenes, notably when Helena's other self sees Koenig again.

The insights into the possible future for the Alphans make this one of the series best.

Definitely a must-see episode for any true fan.

THIS EPISODE:

MISSING LINK

SCREENPLAY - EDWARD DI LORENZO

DIRECTED - RAY AUSTIN

'Missing Link' is not often an episode that makes it into many top ten lists, yet it is one of the richest and most rewarding experiences in the entire series. The pace of the episode is somewhat ponderous with a few slow sections which test the patience, but minor weaknesses notwithstanding, the episode is a truly remarkable one.

There are scenes of suspense, nightmarish horror, and scenes of great beauty too. The planet Zenno is a dreamlike world of light, color and illusion, offering both fears and a life without fear. Perhaps no other episode contains the philosophy of *Space: 1999* and the horror in such equal doses.

The episode kicks off with Koenig's Eagle on the way back from the planet Zenno, escaping a close call. We can assume the star system the Moon has drifted into is in the different area of space it was deposited into by the space time warp at the end of 'Another Time, Another Place'.

The Eagle suddenly goes out of control and crashes, knocking everyone out, Koenig bleeding from a head wound. Director Ray Austin does a great job here as he reveals Koenig is having what seems to be an out of body experience. He has donned a space suit and set off for Alpha, yet his unconscious body is still slumped in the Eagle cabin. The camera work and lighting gives this lengthy sequence a creepy feeling as Koenig finds himself in a deserted Alpha.

While it is a little too long and slow, this part of the episode allows for a great reveal when the entire empty base seems to swirl and evaporate, Koenig finding himself face to face with alien Raan (horror legend Peter Cushing) in his surreal domain on the planet Zenno. Sadly modern high-definition television makes it a little too clear that Zenno is just a big tent with yellow lights and dry ice mist.

This is hard to ignore but despite this, there is much more to enjoy here.

Barry Morse gives one of his most interesting and vivid performance in a scene where Raan makes Koenig think he's awoken back on Alpha. Bergman says what the Alpha crew suspect, that the Moon is their tomb and they're all doomed to die slowly. What's more he outs Koenig as the big man who plays God everyday now they're cut off from Earth.

Morse is terrific and Landau is commendably balanced and rational in response but gets to lose his temper as he realises it is all an illusion created by Raan. The episode immediately jumps to some cracking horror as mutated horror movie freaks come at Koenig from all angles including above.

The camera angles here are like expressionistic cinema and the sequence ends with a desperate, frightened Koenig pleading for help from under a layer of spider web as Victor runs towards him in slow motion, yet never gets closer.

The rest of the episode takes a milder turn with a romantic sub-plot about Koenig and Raan's daughter. But the image of Zenno is one of the most remarkable alien world images in the series and much memorable dialog ensues about this world without fear and the *wonders out there, beyond imagination.*

Special mention should be made of Nick Tate who totally kicks ass in a fight scene where he tries to prevent Helena and Mathias turning off Koenig's life support in Medical Centre. Apparently, Tate accidentally knocked Anton Philips out when a punch connected while they were shooting the fight scene. Philips suffered for his art, but the fight is a great one.

The farewell from Raan to Koenig, after he decides he doesn't want Koenig romancing his daughter and will send him back to Alpha, is also superb as they discuss what they've learned from meeting each other. The ending is terrific too. Helena switches off the life support, grief stricken, but Koenig wakes up and smiles at her.

Yet the question remains, was it real or was his

trip to Zenno all a dream, while he was unconscious from the Eagle crash?

Until tomorrow indeed...

COMPUTER'S OBJECTIVE ASSESSMENT

OVERALL PRODUCTION QUALITY

8/10

The episode is slow and ponderous at times if atmospheric for the most part.

The alien city interior is not so well done compared to what the exterior image suggests.

However, the episode has many highlights along the way, from moments of horror to the superb presence of Peter Cushing. Perhaps most meaningful is the fact that the Alphans, thinking Koenig is dying, seem to fall apart and descend into depression, anger, and even violent outbursts. They need their leader to keep them together, it seems.

Despite plodding along there is much that is rich and rewarding about the episode for the true fan to delve into and appreciate.

THIS EPISODE:

THE GUARDIAN OF PIRI

SCREENPLAY - CHRISTOPHER PENFOLD

DIRECTED - CHARLES CRICHTON

'The Guardian of Piri' may not be the best *Space: 1999* episode but it is certainly one of the most vivid and memorable, featuring a striking guest appearance by future Maya actress Catherine Schell and one of the most original and mesmerizing sets for an alien planet ever to appear in TV Science Fiction as the planet Piri.

It is a truly alien world, a strange, surreal, colourful, and unforgettable place, a world of mountains and mist, a world where the ground is covered by a multi-coloured tiled floor and strange clusters of large and small white spheres rise up on twisted black stalks and stems, or even just hang suspended in the air.

Apparently, the designer based the set on frog spawn. A set for an earlier television series had been based on images of frog spawn and the same idea was reused but with greater impact and scope for the surface of Piri, with its suspended spheres of different sizes. The model work for the episode is skillfully matched to the full-sized set and gives an even greater visual sense of this strange, eerie world.

The episode begins with Alpha already having sent an eagle to investigate the planet following on the heels of 'Missing Link'.

It's entirely plausible that Piri is another planet in the same Criton star system as Raan 's planet of Zenno, further along the trajectory of the Moon's drift.

The moon becomes ensnared by the power of a machine on surface of the planet. Known as the Guardian, it is an enigmatic, ancient machine which captures the moon the way a spider's web might catch a passing fly.

The servant of the Guardian appears in female form. Catherine Schell is immediately striking and memorable as a very attractive female alien with undercurrent of cool menace, and it's not difficult to see why she was asked to return to the series as a regular in the second season, also playing the role of an alien.

Piri is an eerie and creepy place and there are many surreal and spooky sequences involving Alphans standing about in a trance-like state, staring into the sky, and an Eagle suspended in midair.

The Guardian itself has a single white light which shines like an eye on its victims and seems to be a technological counterpart to the hypnotic, single eye of the monster from Dragon's Domain. It is a machine-like Cyclops, a Cthulu-like horror, with Siren-like powers to bend minds and lure space travelers to their doom.

It turns out the people of Piri wanted freedom from decision and obligation and created a machine to induce a state of bliss. This really comes across as a parallel to 60s and 70s Counterculture, dropouts, hippies, and drug users. The whole episode could be taken as a criticism of the Counterculture movement or even an anti-drug message piece. But there is more to the episode than just saying no to drugs and remembering one's responsibilities. Under the influence of 'The Guardian of Piri', the Alphans turn against Koenig, even hospitalizing him like a mental patient. And attentive viewers might pick up on a pun in which two astral bodies, Piri and the Moon, are referred to with the line "best of both worlds", long before it became a famous story title in *Star Trek: The Next Generation*.

This leads to some of the most paranoid and compelling scenes in *Space:1999* as the whole crew of Alpha turn against Koenig. The servant of the Guardian even recites some rather Orwellian lines at Koenig about the need to submit and conform to the prime directive. She also talks about the Pirian goal to find perfection, but Koenig's response about life being transient, imperfect, and temporary are a reminder of why he is very much a hero who fights for humanity and what it means to be human.

In a gripping ending, Koenig fights off laser armed Alphans bent on killing him and after declaring the Pirians must have all died, just as the Alphans are dying, of total apathy, shoots down the servant of the Guardian, revealing her to be a machine.

Her destruction triggers a massive series of explosions and the Alphans wake up and flee the planet in their Eagle fleet.

Piri is set free of its self-imposed curse. Time and life are restored to the surface of the planet, and we see green plant life growing in the sunshine at the end.

While featuring some logic issues, this is one of *Space:1999*'s most haunting, stylish, and unforgettable gems!

COMPUTER'S OBJECTIVE ASSESSMENT

OVERALL PRODUCTION QUALITY

9/10

The story itself has elements which do not make a complete sense such as the Alphans being able to walk around freely both on Alpha and the surface of Piri, despite the claim that Alpha has been immobilised because the Guardian is stopping time.

The Eagles suspended in mid-air look impressive but again this makes very little logical sense.

However the set design and the overall entertainment value of the episode are outstanding as are the sense of menace and the themes being evoked.

Flaws aside, a classic and one example of what makes *Space:1999* so unique.

THIS EPISODE:

FORCE OF LIFE

SCREENPLAY - JOHNNY BYRNE

DIRECTED - DAVID TOMBLIN

Every great television series needs a good head writer to hold it all together and although he did not start out as *Space:1999*'s story editor or head writer, it is Johnny Byrne who ultimately takes on this role of being the backbone of the writing in the series. Before *Space:1999*, the Andersons had relied upon the skills of Tony Barwick from his time expanding half hour episodes of *Thunderbirds* to an hour by adding sub plots to his job as script editor and main contributor on *UFO*. Barwick was not invited to work on *Space:1999* as the American buyers wanted more American input and it is easy to see how this led to Art Wallace of *Star Trek* fame becoming an early contributor.

George Bellak was another man brought in at the start, but despite Bellak, Wallace, and Christopher Penfold's contributions, it was Irish poet turned script writer Johnny Byrne who would contribute about a third of the scripts and do more to shape *Space:1999* than anyone else.

With 'Force of Life', Byrne begins a series of Alpha centric episodes which avoid the question of the

Moon's ability to reach other planets by simply bringing aliens and other menaces to the Moon, from out there in the darkness of space.

Shown in the UK as the second episode, 'Force' is like a *Night Stalker* episode set on Alpha, with a great deal of its plot and imagery owed to Nigel Kneale's The *Quatermass Experiment* as well.

As with *The Night Stalker* series, there is a monster on the loose, racking up victims. But whereas *Night Stalker* took place on contemporary Earth, here the monster of the week is on the loose inside Moon Base Alpha. And as with astronaut Victor Carroon in The *Quatermass Experiment*, it is a possessed human on the loose who is the monster in question, complete with a concerned and distressed wife in tow.

The plot of this episode is actually very simple, with an energy-eating ball of living light blue coming to Alpha, invading, and possessing the body of crewman Anton Zoref, taking him over, infusing him with an insatiable hunger for heat and energy. Koenig and Bergman are forced to investigate a spate of bizarre freezing deaths on the base.

Zoref is a conduit for the alien force to feed with. The force is using him to stalk the corridors, draining power and leaving frozen, ice-covered corpses in his wake.

The whole thing is elevated to classic status by the high quality of the script, direction, lighting, special effects make up and the guest cast. Ian McShane is very good indeed in an early role as the hapless and doomed Anton Zoref.

'Force' is one of a trilogy of bottle episodes set almost entirely on the base, with little or no Eagles, all featuring his gift for horror. The other two are 'The Troubled Spirit' and 'End of Eternity'. All three elevate the suspense and tension with menacing atmosphere aplenty and some awesome horror sequences.

With 'Force of Life', the horror movie elements are in full swing as Zoref accidentally kills his best buddy Dominix while working with him and even breaks into the solarium where young Alphan women are lying around in bikinis.

Director David Tomblin, of *The Prisoner* and *UFO*, pours on the chills with a series of bizarre camera angles that are at times reminiscent of Hitchcock's *Psycho* and Kubrick's *The Shining*. Zoref collapses when the energy creature first invades his body and he falls in slow motion, with a number of jump cuts, the camera then turning until the image of his body is completely upside down, right before the opening titles crash in with their ominous drum roll.

The makeup department are not to be outdone and deliver an amazing transformation of Zoref into a blackened, scorched, smoking corpse that revives as a zombie with unnerving, glowing white eyes. The makeup team on the series gave it a sense of horror that almost eclipsed its impact as space adventure. Zoref's burned body gets back up and the light from his eyes gives the impression he is pure white-hot energy on the inside, as if it is literally blazing out of his eye sockets.

This effect is astonishing and horrible and made a strong impact at the time, no doubt rivalling the monster from 'Dragon's Domain' as the source of many more childhood nightmares. Even modern HD screens cannot diminish how good it is.

COMPUTER'S OBJECTIVE ASSESSMENT

OVERALL PRODUCTION QUALITY

9/10

This episode is a little slow and the scene where the Alphans go into a freeze for a short time in the cold open is little less than totally convincing.

There's also no Eagle action or alien ships for fans of such things to enjoy.

On the other hand, once the episode gets into full swing, the suspense, horror atmosphere, grisly make up effects and big ending all add up to a very compelling episode.

The guest cast all do fine work and it's a great thriller for any sci fi fan to enjoy.

THIS EPISODE:

ALPHA CHILD

SCREENPLAY - CHRISTOPHER PENFOLD

DIRECTED - RAY AUSTIN

The Omen in Space might be a good title for this tale of a scary little boy who terrorises Moon Base Alpha with his psychic influence and seems to plot its downfall.

A baby is born on Alpha and there are tears of joy and happiness, notably from Sandra. Helena is overjoyed at having delivered the baby. But something sinister is approaching from out of the icy depths of space. It looks like a pulsating green ball of light and energy.

Suddenly the mother of the new baby screams in horror and Helena turns to see the baby has transformed into a boy of almost five years! It's a cracking good opening which packs a punch, and we are soon faced with a story which is chilling and confronting, despite being another Penfold script which has many loose plot points and science which doesn't bear too much scrutiny.

First of all, kudos to the director and little Wayne Brooks as five-year-old Jackie, who comes across as a lovely child yet clearly one with a sinister, menacing side. Bergman and Alan get many charming and endearing scenes with little Jackie and when he is dressed like a small Koenig in the same uniform Paul gets to joke about having found a new Commander.

Koenig's doubts about the child are well played by Martin Landau and he gets one of his finest scenes talking about his thoughts on fear and why fear of the unknown is no excuse to start shooting. This suggests the episode should probably be viewed later than 'War Games', as Koenig is always on an extended learning curve in his journey through the Universe and he seems less trigger happy, more considered here than he was in 'War Games' before the aliens taught him their anti-aggression lesson. (Or do the events of 'War Games' simply push him over the edge into desperation?)

Koenig is always the contemporary man who is emotionally and intellectually unprepared for deepest space and all it contains, always forced to learn as he goes, from a cosmic school of hard knocks.

As the story progresses little Jackie begins to exert psychic control over Alan Carter who has shown him the inside of an Eagle.

When alien ships arrive it seems Jackie has been sketching them before their arrival. He gives a knowing look towards the camera which is a very sinister moment. Soon little Jackie transforms into a man, and it is Julian Glover, a superb actor with many celebrated appearances in cult works like *Quatermass and the Pit, Blake's 7, Empire Strikes Back* and *Doctor Who,* (notably 'City of Death') who is typically strong and menacing as alien Jarak.

The alien's wife takes over the body of Jackie's mother and we get the disturbing image of mother and son kissing each other, not as mother and son, but as lovers. Glover's alien exerts psychic control which chokes Dr Mathias in a manner most *Star Wars* fans will recognise as Darth Vader's method of dealing with opposition in the first *Star Wars* movies.

Bain is superb in the scenes where she falls under the influence of the alien. Anton Philips is always great as Dr Mathias, and he really gets to shine in his moments in this episode. When the alien usurpers of the bodies of the baby and his mother reveal they are fugitives, it's not long before their pursuers arrive and deal with them.

This is lucky for the Alphans as they are on the verge of death and bodily possession when this happens. Finally, when the aliens are removed, it is revealed that mother and baby have been restored.

Dr Mathias is in a state of overwhelm, reduced to tears, having just witnessed what seemed like a miracle. It's another example of the series very high level of commitment to realism in human reactions to imaginative situations and quality acting performances in general, which really are noticeable in this episode.

There are a couple of misjudgements. Jarak's costume is a little odd, featuring silver shorts and he also has the ability to impersonate Koenig's voice which seems farfetched. On the other hand, the model space ships, and Eagle action is very well done and as exciting and memorable as ever.

All in all, 'Alpha Child' is a shocking and unsettling excursion into space horror, despite lacking the gory make up effects or dark lighting of some others.

COMPUTER'S OBJECTIVE ASSESSMENT

OVERALL PRODUCTION QUALITY

8/10

The casual viewer may find this a strange episode with the plot where things happen that are difficult to comprehend or understand.

The ending in particular might seem to be a confusing or incomprehensible resolution. The costume for the main villain looks a little bit silly and the Commander's voice being dubbed onto Jarak's mouth is also a bit silly.

However, the model work and visual effects for alien spaceships and Eagles going into action is very well done and looks great, with plenty of laser fire and exploding ships.

The little boy is a good mix of charming and scary and the overall impression is a well-made and engaging episode.

THIS EPISODE:

THE LAST SUNSET

SCREENPLAY - CHRISTOPHER PENFOLD

DIRECTED - CHARLES CRICHTON

'The Last Sunset' is an episode which features a very bold and vivid idea at its core. The premise of the episode is that aliens intervene with life on the moon, causing the moon to become endowed with an oxygen atmosphere, and of course a blue sky, which means the Alphans can breathe out on the surface of the moon.

The idea itself pushes the limits of credibility almost to breaking point, but the end result is such a charming and instantly engaging idea such a marvellous situation, that it would have been a tragedy not to do it.

Apparently, it was Gerry Anderson's idea. Anderson apparently thought he could save money on episode if the sky was blue and the moon suddenly looked like Earth in the modern day, albeit still barren and devoid of trees. However, in reality, executing the idea turned out to be extremely expensive as it required all new special effects sequences done specifically for the episode, depicting Alpha and the Eagles with the blue sky, clouds, etc, instead of the usual black star scape.

One of the great strengths of this episode is the early charm and humour as the Alphans react to their extraordinary new circumstances. Once again *1999* does a great job of conveying the idea that this is intelligent science fiction as we hear the Commander of the base reacting to the situation by describing the blue sky and the red sunrise as indicators of an oxygen atmosphere.

The alien device which places the atmosphere of the moon is small and its capacity seems to be just about infinite despite its size. This might be interesting for fans of the BBC's *Doctor Who* as not only is the device or canister blue, but like the Doctor's blue Police Box, it would have to be bigger on the inside than is on the outside to be able to contain enough oxygen to give the moon an atmosphere.

One thing which is not fully explained is how the moon's gravity increases to the point of becoming like that of Earth, but allowing for the fact that the writers skip over some elements of the story which could do with more explaining, the end result is nevertheless a very exciting and engaging premise. Once again minor and supporting characters such as Paul, Sandra, and the ever-popular Alan, even Tanya, get plenty of great material and once again there is strong hints of a relationship brewing between Paul and Sandra.

The episode as a whole makes a strong companion piece to 'Another Time, Another Place', as it plants the seeds of the possible future seen on the alternative Earth in that story, where Paul and Sandra were married with children. There is a fairly lengthy sequence involving these characters along with Helena Russell stranded after an Eagle crash, too.

This part gets a little bit heavy and depressing for a time, but the cast shine in these scenes, making it tough but rewarding viewing. However, it all turns around in a rousing finale when Paul eats a kind of magic mushroom growing on the moon. These mysterious moon mushrooms with hallucinatory elements, presumably caused by the alien objects which gave the moon its atmosphere, send Paul over the edge and turn him into a raving psychotic loony, who needs to be subdued for the good of all.

With time running out and the atmosphere about to be removed again by the same alien benefactors who bestowed it, the Commander races to the rescue and ends up in a full-on punch-up with the deranged, hallucinating Paul, shortly after he's taken Alan to task.

This part of the plot involves some writing that is unfortunately a little bit embarrassing, in one way, for the series as a whole. Paul's rantings and ravings take the form of claims about destiny, claims about a lack of mere coincidence in events involving Alpha and his belief in a purpose involving Mankind's future. He rambles about these things, wild eyed and scary, and there is a lot of pseudo-Biblical references about Manna from Heaven, a Second Coming and allusions to old

Peru.

While this is fine in itself, it's unfortunate that it happens to be very similar to a lot of the stuff which appears in other episodes of the series where it's presented not as the ravings of a hallucinating lunatic but as genuine, sober, serious conjecture and so this scene kind of flips the Biblical nature of *Space: 1999*'s central theme on its head. If the viewer is prepared to overlook this or will turn a blind eye and suspend their disbelief, then Paul's crazy trip on Moon mushrooms makes for an exciting and dramatic finale, with a great fight sequence.

Helena Russell also gets to be a total bad ass when she blows up the entire crashed Eagle with a well-aimed blast from a laser rifle. The ship's explosion is so big it knocks her backwards off her feet and gets the attention of the Commander's searching Eagle. Once again the Commander gets a great fight scene, flattening the deranged Paul and gets one of the funniest lines when he informs Paul "its moments like that you find out who your friends are!"

There is a surprisingly easy-going attitude towards drugs in this episode, which contradicts the somewhat anti-drug-culture message of 'The Guardian of Piri' episode, as Paul laughs and says that it wasn't a bad trip! Another noteworthy point is that the episode uses a device often used in old episodes of the outer limits as it turns out the aliens gave the humans an atmosphere as a distraction, as a way of confining them to the moon. Why? Because they've seen human history and human nature and they are not impressed with our violent and warlike ways.

They wanted the humans to stay away and not disturb them, because we humans are so destructive they were not prepared to risk meeting any of us. It's a kick in the guts for the humans to be judged so harshly by an alien race who have apparently seen human history since the beginning of time and knows all about its faults and failings as a species. Once again *Space: 1999* proves to be entertaining, imaginative, thought provoking and a show with warmth, humour, suspense, and drama. Unsurprisingly 'The Last Sunset' is something of a fan favourite.

The haunting ending is particularly well done, too. As Paul and Sandra watch the sun setting, this final chance to watch a sunset before they are committed to life in space, is symbolic.

As the sun sets and its red-light fades to darkness, so too their hopes of a new life together, away from Alpha, also fades. It is a bittersweet ending, but it hammers home the significance of Paul and Sandra and their potential future together.

COMPUTER'S OBJECTIVE ASSESSMENT

OVERALL PRODUCTION QUALITY

9/10

This is a well-made episode based on a fascinating premise. The sight of the Moon with the blue sky and breathable atmosphere is fascinating to any viewer and immediately arrests the attention.

The first half of the episode is charming and intriguing. Paul and Sandra in particular get some great material which develops their romance and Paul also gets to cause a lot of trouble.

The ending is exciting, with plenty of fight scene action and it remains a popular episode with fans who want to know more about the Alphans as people.

THIS EPISODE:

VOYAGER'S RETURN

SCREENPLAY - JOHNNY BYRNE

DIRECTED - BOB KELLETT

'Voyager's Return' is one of the more realistic storylines of *Space: 1999* and one of the most powerful. In fact, 'Voyager's Return' may just be the best episode of *Space: 1999* of them all.

The episode is not perfect, it does have its flaws, but Johnny Byrne typically has a stronger grasp of science fiction than most writers working on the series around him and makes a genuine effort to explain the ability of the Voyager probe to traverse great distances by giving it an experimental form of interstellar propulsion or star-drive known as the Queller Drive.

This engine is named after its creator but sadly for him and others, not only does the Queller Drive (attempt to) justify the ability of Voyager to traverse interstellar space but it is lethal.

The drive system is absolutely central to the story itself in fact because the deadly power of the Queller Drive makes it very much a weapon of mass destruction, a metaphor for pollution as well as Man's propensity for destroying his environment and, in his ignorance, inflicting death upon other species of life.

Even his fellow members of the human race have paid a price in this case. Some contrivances in the story may make viewers wonder, while the capabilities of the drive itself may not hold up too closely to logical scrutiny. However these criticisms aside, the episode contains considerable dramatic power, strong characterisation, strong dialogue, excellent pacing and an outstanding ending and story resolution.

The character of Ernst Queller is perhaps best summed up by the old saying he and Helena Russell discuss in the Medical Centre which says *the road to hell is paved with good intentions*.

Queller's good intentions, when he explains them, almost sound like a rewrite of the opening narration of *Star Trek* as he talks about illuminating the mysteries of science, exploring the depths of space, discovering new civilisations, and offering hand friendship.

Queller's story is a dire warning about misguided idealism and how the best intentions can backfire and perhaps a suggestion that no good deed goes unpunished in an indifferent universe. Queller's presence on Alpha leads to a story of guilt and redemption. First comes the guilt.

The episode begins with a startling cold open. Two Eagles head out in front of Alpha into the black void of space. Something is coming at them out of the emptiness, something dangerous and mysterious. Suddenly a call sign is heard: "This is the voice of Voyager 1."

Professor Bergman's reaction is one of sheer horror as he identifies a Voyager ship. Immediately picking up on the danger, Koenig orders the Eagles to pull out. Alan Carter wrestles with his controls, stating "we're under attack."

The sequence involves the use of a rapid zoom lens movement, in and out, creating a pulsating affect, to suggest the impact of the Queller Drive upon two Eagles.

Alan barely manages to get away, while the pilot of the other Eagle is cut off in the middle of screaming "oh my God." And, in a moment of great stunt work, is seen being sucked out of his seat, over the console and presumably out into space just a split-second before his Eagle blows to smithereens.

This is the kind of chilling sense of nuclear destruction in the icy blackness of space that left a lasting impression on viewers. With the Eagle destroyed, the Alphans can only stare and listen in disbelief as the calm, sonorous voice from space announces, "this is the voice of Voyager 1... greetings from the people of the planet Earth."

Some greetings! And Landau and Bain's looks of silent horror, their eyes widening, is priceless.

The opening titles sequence and its thunderous dramatic music crashes in as we realize this craft from Earth brings nothing but death and destruction. The Alphans are initially torn by conflict over what to do about the Voyager. Paul describes vividly the threat of the fast neutrons spewed out into space which propel Voyager across interstellar distances at fantastic speeds. He says even if they climbed into lead caskets under 50 feet of concrete, they would still be burned up, a graphic and scary description.

Victor Bergman on the other hand takes the scientist's approach, getting enthusiastic about the knowledge the space probe may have acquired out there in deepest space. Koenig seems to listen to Victor's ideas about trying to save Voyager and land it safely on Alpha, rather than simply destroying this dangerous machine. And this brings us to one of Barbara Bain's most scathing, sarcastic lines as she coldly remarks "I guess we better find out everything we can... about fast neutrons!"

The episode then reveals the creator of the probe and its deadly engine, Dr Ernst Queller, is on the base under a false name. This is a beautifully written guest character and the guest star who plays the part, Jeremy Brett, turns in a likeable and sympathetic performance as a well-meaning but enormously tragic figure.

It further transpires that another Voyager ship malfunctioned on takeoff, causing the destruction of the entire community on Earth. This incident made Queller's name less than mud.

The incident also cost the life of Paul Morrow's parents and the parents of Queller's assistant Jim, leading to some moments of emotional tension.

Queller undertakes to reprogram Voyager and turn off the Queller Drive. He succeeds but not before his assistant Jim has realised that he is working with the infamous Professor Queller, turned on him in a fit of angry rage and knocked him down.

Alpha is spared annihilation from the Queller drive and Dr Queller succeeds in landing his probe at the base. However, there is another twist to the story; the probe has been followed through space by a fleet of alien warships. In another triumph for *Space:1999*, the alien ships bear an uncanny resemblance to metal insects, like angry hornets or bees, ready to sting their opponents to death.

The Alphans receive a holographic message from the alien leader, Aarchon, (Alex Scott in a cold, measured and menacing performance) and in one of the most sharply written pieces of dialogue in the series, the alien leader outlines the fact that the Queller drive caused all life on two of the aliens' planets to be extinguished. Now they are following the Voyager, seeking justice and retribution. They intend to find its planet of origin, Earth, and destroy it in retaliation. And of course, they will destroy Alpha on the way!

Queller is overwhelmed with guilt and regret and goes up into outer space to confront the aliens by piloting Voyager probe like a spaceship. He intends to reason with the aliens, but his efforts are to no avail. When his request that they punish him and not a bunch of innocent people for his mistakes, his plea is rejected.

The fatalistic Professor Queller gets another one of *1999*'s all-time classic lines: "if you would destroy an entire world to punish the mistakes of one man then you are no more worthy of life than I am."

He uses the Queller driver as a weapon against alien fleet, blasting them with short bursts of fast neutrons, then he heads in and operates the probe 's self-destruct, giving his life to destroy the alien fleet and save Alpha and Earth.

The parallels between Queller and the creator of the atomic bomb must be obvious. The themes of guilt, regret, taking responsibility for one's actions and attempting to redeem oneself for past mistakes, these things are what makes the episode resonate with so much power.

The episode also tells us something about Koenig. Unlike Straker of *UFO*, Koenig does not see things in stark black and white terms. He is a much more fluid and changeable character, and in this situation, he is willing to gamble on Queller to get the Voyager down safely. Later, when facing an alien threat, we see him deny he is a betting man, longing instead for a second chance. For Koenig, learning as he goes in uncharted space, taking risks or playing it safe seems to be on a case by case basis and this enables Landau to develop a subtle and complex performance.

And did this episode influence *Star Trek: The Motion Picture*, which used the real-life Voyager probe as the basis of its V'Ger? The movie has a cold atmosphere which could imply some *Space:1999* Year One influence.

All in all, 'Voyager's Return' is one of the most gripping, compelling, and potent episodes of TV science-fiction ever broadcast and truly one of the best episodes of *Space: 1999* as a whole.

COMPUTER'S OBJECTIVE ASSESSMENT

OVERALL PRODUCTION QUALITY

10/10

While some might question the science and logic of a probe which can scour the galaxy in 15 years and has seats and oxygen supply so Queller can pilot it into space like a spaceship, 'Voyager's Return' in a totally gripping episode with potent themes of guilt and redemption, great acting from the guest cast and a riveting script.

The ending is powerful and haunting and there's plenty of good space model work to excite as well.

It may lack the horror of some of the other great episodes, but for sheer story power, this one is hard to beat.

THIS EPISODE:

COLLISION COURSE

SCREENPLAY - ANTHONY TERPILOFF

DIRECTED - RAY AUSTIN

'Collision Course' kicks off with one of the show's most riveting cold opens, a gripping slice of pure space drama with the Eagles in action and Alan Carter in full heroic mode as a huge asteroid threatens to destroy moon base unless the Alphans can destroy it first.

A fleet of Eagles is busy carrying nuclear mines out into space and clamping them to the asteroid. But all is not well. Alan's Eagle is malfunctioning, and time is running out. Koenig gives Alan a little more time, but he is risking Alpha.

Alan completes his mission by sheer guts and determination, but he lacks adequate time to escape. Believing he has sent Alan to his doom; Koenig is in tears as the nukes explode and the asteroid vaporises.

Martin Landau is a little heavy handed in his performance but leaves us with no doubt that Koenig sees this situation as one of life and death. He also pours on the drama as he stresses in the aftermath of the explosion, wondering if Alan is dead and refusing to face the possibility that he has gotten Alan killed.

But Alan is not dead. A mysterious presence has intervened to save him and guides Koenig and Paul to him. But a new discovery shocks them. The moon is on a collision course with a huge planet. As with 'Earthbound', the writer displays the skills which made him a contributor to Hitchcock's TV anthology. The tension mounts as the Alphans devise a plan to lay a nuclear mine field in space, hoping to detonate it to change the Moon's course.

But Koenig has an encounter in space with an alien ship and meets a woman called Arra and has a remarkable conversation with her. 'Collision Course' contains some of the most memorable and meaningful dialog in the whole series. The actress Margaret Leighton who plays Arra was dying when the episode was being made. It is very sad to think this was her last acting performance.

However, we can take solace in the fact that she gives an absolutely outstanding performance as the alien queen who imparts wisdom and knowledge of the universe to the Commander. It is a performance for which she can be remembered as a great actress.

This episode is the second in the trilogy which deals with the mysterious undefined force which was first mentioned in the 'Black Sun'. Koenig asks for specific information, and he is told that the Alphans have a destiny to go into deepest space, that their odyssey will know no end and they will colonise the farthest reaches of space. Their children will colonise worlds without number. If she is right, the journey of the Alphans has a clear purpose now. But is Arra telling him the truth? The Alphans do not think so, but Koenig seemingly has faith in her.

On Arra's instructions, Koenig attempts to convince the Alphans to do nothing and allow the Moon and Arra's planet to collide in space. Taking her at her word, Koenig insists the Alphans allow the collision and do nothing, but they do not take this idea lying down.

The ending of this episode is amazingly tense and suspenseful as the moon comes very close to being destroyed once again but this time it seems to be a miracle of sorts which saves the base.

Landau is terrific in this finale as he seems genuinely scared out of his wits as he watches the planet approach and shouts at Bergman that he believed Arra, as their time appears to be running out fast.

The planet vanishes at the point of contact with the moon. The commander is stunned by this experience and is left to ponder what he went through. Landau and Tate deliver stellar performances in the tense confrontation scene in the climax. It seems Koenig's faith is being tested and it is unnerving to experience.

In all this is a remarkable episode with a fabulous

script and brilliant acting and direction. There are some lapses in space science and physics, around the idea of Operation Shockwave, but these are minor considerations in view of the sheer potency of the plotline as a whole and the skill with which it is performed and directed.

As a piece of television drama, it is a fabulous episode with a brilliant ending and some of the series most important, resonant, and potent dialogue.

COMPUTER'S OBJECTIVE ASSESSMENT

OVERALL PRODUCTION QUALITY

10/10

This test of faith story is very well done and features a great guest performance and highly memorable dialog. Koenig's faith seems to grow stronger out of this experience and we see why he is the one who holds Alpha together in deep space.

The tension and suspense of the climax is acted and directed with great power and the ending is really astonishing.

The science and physics behind operation shockwave are rather questionable, but this is a quibble compared to the overall power of the storyline.

THIS EPISODE:

DEATH'S OTHER DOMINION

**SCREENPLAY - ANTHONY TERPILOFF
&
ELIZABETH BARROWS**

DIRECTED - CHARLES CRICHTON

Although it is not seen on screen, it is mentioned during the course of the episode that the Moon may have passed through yet another time warp at some point before its arrival in the star system which contains the planet known as Ultima Thule, in the episode 'Death's Other Dominion'.

This time warp would be the third we know of since the events of the break away and the planet featured in this episode appears to be a cold outer planet of its star system, a brutal and punishing environment which is covered in a layer of snow and ice.

Once again production standards are amazing, and the ice planet is created in studio to vivid and memorable effect. It is a planet which almost kills the Alphans when they first go down, too, with Alan struggling back to the Eagle after the regulars are lost in a deadly blizzard.

The script for this episode is exceptionally good,

featuring strong characters and rich dialogue, some of which seems to have been inspired by the works of William Shakespeare. The guest cast as usual a very high calibre. Brian Blessed and John Shrapnel both turn in excellent performances and the plot seems to have been inspired by the story *The Lost Horizon* as the planet and its human colony is much like the mythical Shangri-La .

There is an underground colony of humans who have survived from a space probe which originally left Earth with the intention of exploring the planet Uranus. Once again the series suggests that forces in space carried humans much further than expected, depositing them onto this far-flung world.

But this explanation it comes with a twist. Since arriving on the planet the human survivors have not aged a day, they have become immortal .

Once again, we see that Koenig is the type of leader we would want in charge in real life because nothing persuades him to agree to anything which could be dangerous to his people. In stark contrast to 'Voyager's Return' and 'Matter of Life and Death', Koenig is not prepared to take risks in this episode, viewing the situation on Ultima Thule with skepticism which only builds the more he learns.

'Dominion' is a companion piece in many ways to 'End of Eternity'. Both episodes deal with the subject of immortality that come at it from different angles. The script for this episode is particularly rich and contains wonderful dialogue.

There is something rather Shakespearean about the fool and it seems as if the writer is drawing from Shakespeare's *King Lear*. In *King Lear*, the fool is the one who is wise. The story is fascinating for the way it depicts the Commander struggling through a maze of small and subtle discoveries to find the real truth about the situation on the ice planet.

Guided by a wise fool, Koenig eventually finds his way to an understanding which his own people are not willing to accept until the truth is shown to them in the shock ending of the story.

Brian Blessed had not yet become famous for his larger-than-life acting performance in the movie *Flash Gordon* in which he played the king of the Hawk men and delivered the famous line "Gordon's Alive".

In this episode Blessed is remarkably restrained and convincing as a thoughtful but utterly misguided scientist. Immortality, which has been one of the great human quests since the writing of the *Epic of Gilgamesh*, is once more depicted as a pipe dream not worth pursuing.

Death is once again affirmed as the only thing which can give true meaning to life. It's an absorbing and thought-provoking episode with magnificent sets and a great guest cast. The special effects department deliver some interesting shots of Alan trying to get his Eagle out of the ice and snow, too. But it is the visual effects make up which really steals the episode in the end.

The final twist of the episode provides another example of *Space:1999*'s mind blowing grasp of horror. This comes as Blessed's self-assured character Dr Rowland leaves the planet and its zone of influence in an Eagle, intent of trying to convince the Alphans to come and live on Thule, only to be transformed instantly into an eight-hundred-year-old skeleton and some steaming, dead remains!

The fact he's holding Helena's hand at the time is enough to give anyone bad dreams, too.

A poetic, haunting and classy episode, 'Death's Other Dominion' is one of *Space: 1999*'s very finest accomplishments.

COMPUTER'S OBJECTIVE ASSESSMENT

OVERALL PRODUCTION QUALITY

10/10

A rich script and outstanding guest cast and alien planet settings give this fable of a lost paradise real class.

The dialog is a delight, and the themes are deep and dark.

This is possibly one of *Space:1999*'s finest ever achievements and the ending is yet another brilliant and unforgettable twist, a proper sting in the tail.

THIS EPISODE:

THE FULL CIRCLE

SCREENPLAY - JESSE LASKY JNR
&
PAT SILVER

DIRECTED - BOB KELLETT

The biggest failure of any episode of this otherwise amazingly good series arrives in 'The Full Circle', yet in a series which has treated the explanations with ambiguity and restraint, it just about gets away with it. Just about, but not quite.

There is no logical reason for the crew of Moon base Alpha to be transformed into Stone Age people on the planet Retha, and even Bergman mentioning a time warp is not adequate this time.

Yet, despite this, we still get a generally compelling and entertaining episode with plenty to enjoy. The cold open is another good one, beginning with an Eagle already on the surface of a new planet and the Commander worrying about the team who went down and have failed to report back on time.

The planet Retha is a verdant and primitive world and great model work is expertly matched with the series' first extensive use of location filming. Black Park Lake, often used in *UFO*, doubles for Retha and the Alphan costumes make a rather surreal impression on location.

Alan, Victor, Paul, and Kano get a lot of good dialog and character moments here. But Sandra is the real star here. Ziennia Merton gets to switch into a furry animal skin costume and earns her stripes as *Space: 1999*'s scream queen.

Alan is heroic as ever, here, relatable for his concern for Sandra and determination to rescue her when she is dragged away by Stone Age savages and tied up in a cave. Barbara Bain almost steals the crown for screaming at one point.

Shaking off her icy performances as Dr Russell and giving anyone who thinks she's wooden something to consider, Bain goes absolutely nuts shrieking like a wild banshee as her cave woman incarnation when Sandra hits cave man Koenig in the head with a rock.

The reveal that all the cave people on Retha are the Alphans themselves is a fun one, but it really needs a better explanation.

It's like a trick a character like *Star Trek*'s Q might play on a space crew to teach them a lesson. It's far too oddball for the Mysterious Undefined Force alluded to in 'Black Sun'.

For all the frustration this invokes, the episode has a satisfying resolution and makes nice points about how modern humans compare to their Stone Age counterparts.

It even ends on a joke made by Commander Koenig

and the Alphans' laughing faces.

If it had been screened early, it may have left a different impression on critics, since it's an episode which displays a level of warmth and humour many other episodes lack.

Sadly, for the series, 'The Full Circle' has become the least popular episode of *Space:1999*, even managing to be less popular with audiences than the worst outings of season 2. This outcome seems a little unfair as the episode, while clearly hurt by a major flaw, is more than competent in most other aspects.

While it may join the likes of 'Ring Around the Moon' and 'Space Brain' in being something of a guilty pleasure, it is worth watching all the same. One interesting point to consider is that the plot has some similarities to the final outing of the BBC's original 1963-1989 production of *Doctor Who*, the story "Survival." In the serial, humans who find themselves on the surface of a primitive and savage planet are slowly transformed both physically and mentally into savage cat-like hunters known as the Cheetah people.

The episode suggests, somewhat loosely, or vaguely, that there is a connection between the planet itself and what happens to the humans who visit it. Perhaps this might help us form a more charitable reading and understanding of 'The Full Circle'.

COMPUTER'S OBJECTIVE ASSESSMENT

OVERALL PRODUCTION QUALITY

6/10

The basic premise of a cave man story seems like a contractual obligation considering the series was inspired in part by *2001* and the Dawn of Man chapter of that movie involved primitive Man.

The location shoot looks good, pacing is generally good and Zienia Merton leaves a strong impression in an unusual role for Sandra.

Sadly, the lack of a coherent explanation for the plot leaves many with the impression this is *Space:1999*'s one true failure. There is some fun to be had from the episode, despite this.

THIS EPISODE:

END OF ETERNITY

SCREENPLAY - JOHNNY BYRNE

DIRECTED - RAY AUSTIN

Jumping into the middle of the investigation by the Alphans of a drifting asteroid in close proximity to the Moon, the story kicks off with astronauts on the asteroid and an Eagle parked on it, at a very steep angle, a classy set up if ever there was one. Bergman suspects there is more than meets the eye here and it's soon confirmed the asteroid contains an atmosphere source.

The Alpha astronauts blast away part of the asteroid surface revealing a hatch and as it opens the opening sequence commences. What follows is one of the series most gripping suspense thrillers.

This is the second of Byrne's trilogy of bottle episodes featuring a menace on the base and this one is defined in dialogue as a killer who can't be friends killed, an immortal man who is imprisoned in the hollow asteroid. The asteroid prison itself is defined magnificently by Bergman as "a one room world ".

The episode once again showcases the talent and presence of its main guest star, in this case Peter

Bowles. To say Bowles dominates the episode is an understatement.

Clad in black and with his feet blocked up for extra height, he breathes life and menace into Balor, a sadistic alien psychopath who tosses Alpha security guards about like rag dolls and takes laser beam hits without flinching. Artful direction here makes his early scenes extra eerie as his fights are presented without sound, just (disturbing) incidental music.

The episode eventually comes down to a one on one contest between Balor and Koenig. There is a mildly amusing moment when the two men stand still and stare at each other in Main Mission, the camera zooming in on their faces, rather like adversaries in a 70s Kung Fu movie.

Nevertheless, this leads to a truly tense and satisfying showdown in the end. One of the other fascinating aspects of the episode involves the character of Baxter played by Australia's Jim Smilie.

Landau actually says "excuse me, Jim" early on, too, calling him by his real name, rather than his character name. Baxter is an astronaut who is grounded permanently after an explosion damages his optic nerve.

Balor visits the depressed Baxter and tampers with his mind, inducing a lethal psychotic episode. The victim is Koenig, who is wounded fatally, only to be healed by Balor somehow sharing his power of cellular regeneration to him.

A shocking image of Koenig face down in a pool of his own blood was cut from the episode but the scene is shocking enough without it.

Thematically we might consider the name Byrne gives to Balor's planet, Progron. Is he talking about progress? Technology and medical progress?

If so, this alien race went down a very dark alley in their pursuit of a medical and biological fountain of youth, creating a callous psychopath with little mercy and no empathy for the mere mortals.

The solution to the idea of an immortal who can regenerate his body and never die turns out to be simple but effective. Balor still requires oxygen to function, so Koenig tricks him into an airlock.

After a tense confrontation, Balor is ejected into the space vacuum where he will presumably become inert and dormant, if not actually die.

All in all, this is a Terminator style thriller on Alpha with a direct and gripping plot and the series adds to its reputation for horror in space.

In many respects this is also one of *Space:1999*'s very best episodes and certainly remains one of its most popular with fans for obvious and vivid reasons.

COMPUTER'S OBJECTIVE ASSESSMENT

OVERALL PRODUCTION QUALITY

9/10

With minimal Eagle action and set mostly on the base, this episode is a little slow to get moving, but once it takes off, there's plenty of action involving the sinister and creepy alien Balor.

A simple, tightly made, and gripping thriller, this is one of the series best hours.

THIS EPISODE:

WAR GAMES

SCREENPLAY - CHRISTOPHER PENFOLD

DIRECTED - CHARLES CRICHTON

'War Games' is an episode which peaks early with a first half which features an all-out rock 'em, sock 'em, alien attack upon Moon Base Alpha, with the heroic Alan and his Eagle fleet taking on the sexiest ships on TV, the Mark 9 Hawks. Looking like a variation on Alpha's super cool Eagles with an added dose of cool and a load of bad ass thrown in for good measure, the Hawks remains one of the most popular one-off creations ever to appear in an Anderson production, particularly with fans who like to build models, produce art or CGI animation. And who can blame them?

Soon Moon base Alpha is destroyed by the attacking alien fleet and only Alan stands in the way of a gigantic alien bomber on its way to deliver the final deathblow. In his crippled and drifting Eagle, with his laser maximum rate, Alan is able to blast alien bomber out of the sky in one of the series most exciting and spectacular sequences.

All of which raises the question: did *Space:1999* inspire George Lucas to make *Star Wars*?

The short answer is probably yes.

The shot of the alien bomber is very reminiscent of the famous opening shot of *Star Wars*. The first half of the episode creates such a dazzling sense of the sheer excitement, drama, and futuristic spectacle of a space war that it's easy to see how a film maker could look at it and think this could be the next big thing. There was also a claim that the original design for Han Solo's Millenium Falcon was changed because it looked too much like a *Space:1999* Eagle ship.

There are also rumours that Lucas visited the *Space:1999* FX studio. The fact that *1999*'s FX wizard Brian Johnson did the FX for *Empire Strikes Back* a little later on may be the smoking gun. Or is it the fact that if you remove the year 1999 and the word "game" from the title *Space:1999* - 'War Games' becomes "Space Wars"?

The devastation of Alpha by the alien fleet is truly shocking and comes complete with stunt men depicting the Alphans being sucked out into space as the base is breached.

In the second half, John and Helena visit the alien planet to confront its leaders and plead for mercy. When the aliens prove aloof and indifferent, Koenig becomes angry, insisting that someone or something is watching over the Alphans in their fight for survival, perhaps God.

Anthony Valentine, well known at the time for co-starring with Edward Woodward in *Callan*, plays the cold, stilted and seemingly indifferent male alien. Isla Blair, whose other TV science fiction roles include *Doctor Who*, *Blake's 7* and The *Quatermass Experiment*, plays the calm and serene female alien.

Both are good if unexciting as the aliens who dismiss the humans as an inferior race, plagued by fears and ultimately doomed. Their damning judgement of humanity provokes Koenig to become enraged in a way rarely seen in the hero of a TV series, even to the point of becoming violent.

Special mention needs to go to Barry Morse here for his epic monolog about the fate of Mankind and the need to learn a lot more. It is a tremendous speech, and he is brilliant. Bergman is an unusual scientist, explaining the fate of Alpha with a reference to the ancient notion of the Gods using humanity for their sport. His dialog in his big speech about how "Man still has much to learn" is marvellous.

This episode is perhaps evidence that a plethora of exciting and expensive special effects can serve to get an audience's attention and then, once viewers are hooked, there is also room for great actors to shine too, with great dialog. The space battles got the "bums on seats" as they say in the theatre, Morse then delivers acting to make it more than just a fireworks display.

Helena is kept by the aliens and learns that these

beings have created a world without fear, much like Zenno. And like the Ariel people of 'Last Sunset', they distrust human nature. Koenig eventually blows up the alien city and unleashes a nuclear holocaust.

This thematic contrast between humans and aliens, underlining how humanity's biggest problem is its own fears, while suggesting that aliens might have achieved some form of enlightenment, seems to be a popular theme in *Space:1999* and perhaps part of the series' philosophy. Fear is the real enemy which Koenig must face and overcome.

Finally, the end seems to come for the Alphans and Landau has a fascinating monolog about his body ending up a piece for some alien archaeologist to find and ponder about in the far future.

But it turns out the battle was in the mind. The aliens showed the Alphans what would happen if they resorted to violence and gave in to fear.

The antiwar and anti-aggression message is a strong one and leaves a lasting impact. Science Fiction taking an anti-war stance is in the long tradition of American series like *Twilight Zone* and *Star Trek*, but rarely has any TV show rendered the theme with such spectacular visual style and power.

'War Games', like 'Dragon's Domain', is not flawless, suffering a tendency to be stilted and slow in its second half, but Bain really shines here, and Nick Tate and Barry Morse also have great moments, with Landau also pushing the envelope as he confronts the aliens. Overall, the story but has enough vivid, impactful sequences and such a potent anti-war theme, it ends up as one of the series greatest achievements.

COMPUTER'S OBJECTIVE ASSESSMENT

OVERALL PRODUCTION QUALITY

8/10

Brian Johnson and Nick Allder's finest hour as they dazzle the audience with space battles galore. There are some cardboard cut outs in use at times and even the wires show up when watched in High Definition, on one model shot, but the sheer impact of their work is hard to deny.

There's also some stiff aliens and stilted acting and some stock footage of H-bomb explosions. On the other hand, the regulars act their socks off, there's some sublime dialog, the moral theme is powerful and the stunt work of Alphans sucked into space is superb.

Koenig makes it plain that he has faith in the human spirit and a belief that someone is watching over the Alphans and we see both his strength and his weaknesses, as he is forced to learn a lesson about violence and aggression. This one is more good than bad, by a considerable distance.

THIS EPISODE:

THE LAST ENEMY

SCREENPLAY - BOB KELLETT

DIRECTED - BOB KELLETT

'The Last Enemy' begins with a very strong opening in which we establish there are two planets on opposite sides of their sun.

They are unable to see each other, however. This situation is reminiscent of the idea of the two Earths which were not aware of each other's existence because they were in the same orbit, on opposite sides of the sun in the Gerry and Sylvia Anderson movie *Doppelgänger*, released in United States under the title *Journey to the Far Side of the Sun*.

Apparently the main idea for the episode came from actress Barbara Bain. The premise seems to be a parallel to the Cold War situation between Russia and the United States which had existed since the 1950s and would remain a big issue in the world until the end of the Cold War in 1989 with the coming down of the Berlin Wall and the collapse of the Soviet Union.

The colours of the planets are red and blue. This is seemingly a reflection of the idea of Russia and

Communism being strongly associated at the time with the colour red.

One of the interesting things about the episode is that the leader of the attacking planet Betha, and the captain of the ship they send to the moon, Captain Dione, and her crew, are all women. However, this is more like a misdirection if anything as the episode actually does not get into gender politics or a *battle of the sexes* situation.

Instead, it focuses on the plight of the moon caught in a similar position to the small countries who feel as if they are helpless victims caught in the middle of the Cold War between the two superpowers of the United States and Russia. This was very topical and current at the time.

The position of the moon and the Alphans probably mirrors the position of Great Britain watching the United States and Russia in the Cold War and hoping not to end up as a casualty in the crossfire of two military giants. There is insufficient evidence in the episode that the planet Delta is male dominated. But the leader is a male and the rival planets leader is female.

A spaceship containing the female captain and her female crew of three comes to the moon to cause trouble. The male leader of the planet Delta was apparently played originally by actor Alan Bennion who was known for playing an Ice Warrior leader on *Doctor Who*.

For some reason, his scenes were removed and re-cast and re-shot. Actor Kevin Stoney, who was also known for many major appearances on *Doctor Who* and other science fiction series made in England, replaced the original male leader.

Stoney was well known to sci fi fans in the UK for playing Dalek ally Mavic Chen and Cyber Men ally Tobias Vaughn with the first two *Doctor Who* incarnations. He would later appear in *The Quatermass Conclusion*, *Blake's 7* and much more.

His role in 'Last Enemy' is a small but impressive part. With his snow-white hair and his habit of lolling back in his seat with his eyes closed as talks, he looks very much like one of the Russian leaders of the Cold War, such as Boris Yeltsin or Mikhail Gorbachev who became to prominence in the 1980s.

In one of the most startling moments in the episode Stoney suddenly opens his eyes and leans toward the camera and shouts *there can be no neutrality!*

Caroline Mortimer makes a strong impression Dione, the main guest role. Her character seems to develop some genuine feelings of affection for Koenig before ultimately betraying him. In fact, even when she is attacking her enemies near the end and thinking Koenig is approaching in a moon buggy, she implores him to take cover as missiles zero in.

We also get the impression Commander begins to feel some genuine affection for her before he is regretfully forced to take action to destroy her.

The ending of this episode was notoriously under running at the time it was made. The entire ending is an add-on to extend the running time, probably written by Johnny Byrne, not the writer whose name is on the episode.

It is this final sequence in which Koenig acts like he's gone mad and wants to betray his friends on Alpha and rush off to Dione's ship to ask for refuge, only to blow it up with the remote-control bomb inside a moon buggy, which actually elicits most of the suspense in the episode.

The novelisation of the episode features the original ending in which Koenig simply tells Kevin Stoney's character the location coordinates of the gunship and she's taken out by a missile strike.

The new ending is much more memorable, if a little obvious, and gives us a very memorable moment when Commander Koenig's space-suited figure, sitting in the moon buggy, drives over a bump on his helmet falls off revealing nothing underneath.

He has no head!

A moment where our heroes head seems to fall off with nothing underneath was a shock and very memorable.

The Commanders line *you only have yourself to blame* is a very good one. The episode elicits happy memories of an exciting situation early on as a gigantic alien ship is moving in on the moon and all of Alpha's Eagles are neutralised, the heroic Alan Carter seen struggling with his ship, the fleet of Eagles blasting their engines, giving off great clouds of steam, but none will take off, just sitting on the launchpads helplessly.

The overall episode is a space opera piece featuring plenty of spaceships, missiles, explosions, and suspense. It's very tense in places and special mention should be given to the female Commissioner, Thea, who comes out with one of the show's funniest ever lines when she says *we are fighting a war - please be brief!*

COMPUTER'S OBJECTIVE ASSESSMENT

OVERALL PRODUCTION QUALITY

9/10

'The Last Enemy' is a cracking good piece of space opera. They're a model spaceships and rockets galore in this episode as well as plenty of explosions and loads of action.

The female villain with her crew of black clad models make for an appealing adversarial.

While there is no horror element there's enough suspense and interesting character interaction between the Commander in the main villain to hold the attention.

For sheer enjoyment is one of the most fun episodes of the entire series.

THIS EPISODE:

THE TROUBLED SPIRIT

SCREENPLAY - JOHNNY BYRNE

DIRECTED - RAY AUSTIN

As previously noted, writer Johnny Byrne had a love of ghost stories and often allowed this to filter into his work on *Space:1999*, notably with Lee Russel in 'Matter of Life and Death' and Regina's doppelganger in 'Another Time, Another Place', but it is with 'Troubled Spirit' that Byrne really lets the ghost story land full force on Moon base Alpha.

Featuring creepy, eerie atmosphere and an unsettling use of coral sitar music, this is Johnny Byrne's most fully realized ghost story for *Space:1999*.

The episode kicks off with a very visual cold open, featuring a lot of lengthy shots in which the camera travels through the corridors of the moon base. Soon, the camera settles upon the sight of a trio of Alphans holding a type of seance. But this is no ordinary seance and moments later, a powerful invisible force is released.

Now, when *Space:1999* went to its second season a lot of fans were very disappointed with the changes brought in by the new producer Fred

Freiberger.

One of three episodes he wrote under a penname involved the Commander talking to three sentient trees on the planet Luton. But while we may laugh at the idea of the brave Commander talking to trees, it should be pointed out that this episode, 'Troubled Spirit', begins with a kind of seance where people sit in a circle around what appears to be a shrub growing in a small container of soil.

The main guest character in this episode, Mateo, wants to establish communication between humans and plants. He and his friends hold this seance style meeting around a shrub to attempt to communicate with plants.

After seeing members of the Moon base crew trying to communicate with plants, it is not a very big leap to imagine that the Commander would eventually meet talking trees in the second season. Oddly enough very few fans of the series ever seem to mention or talk about the rather loopy idea of trying to establish psychic communication with the shrub in this episode.

Even though the episode begins with such an oddball concept, what follows from it is exceptionally atmospheric and creepy and frankly, downright scary. Johnny Byrne delivers the closest thing yet to a genuine ghost story in the science fiction setting of the Moon base with this episode.

Apparently, there was a legend in Byrne's

hometown when he was a child, which involved an old building, said to be haunted.

The story went that if you ran around it fast enough, you would eventually encounter yourself. This idea of the ghostly doppelganger had appeared with Regina in 'Another Time, Another Place' and it is here again with Mateo haunted by his own, horrific double.

The man who would communicate with a shrub passes out and as soon haunted by what appears to be his own ghost which was somehow come back in time from the future from after the time of his death.

Anyone who gets in his way or annoys him or frustrates him is soon struck down by the murderous wrath of 'The Troubled Spirit'. A great deal of the success of this episode is down to the way it is produced and directed.

The director pours on the creepy and spooky atmosphere while the production team delivers some genuinely shocking and grizzly make-up effects for the horribly disfigured ghost double.

One of the joys of this episode is watching the Professor play an exorcist and try to carry out sci-fi exorcism to get rid of the ghost.

Overall 'The Troubled Spirit' turns out to be a gripping and thought-provoking episode. Incidentally, Byrne would later write for *Doctor*

Who, including Arc of Infinity, in which the Doctor would face a doppelganger of himself which begins to decay and turn horrific.

Some aspects of the plot are highly ambiguous or just not explained. But despite these weaknesses the episode is a vivid and memorable ghost story.

Along with 'Force of Life' and 'End of Eternity' it makes up a trilogy of Moon based stories which rely on suspense and spooky atmosphere instead of action and special effects to carry the hour.

This trilogy of Moon based horror stories is definitely one of the highlights of the first season, talking with shrubs notwithstanding.

COMPUTER'S OBJECTIVE ASSESSMENT

OVERALL PRODUCTION QUALITY

9/10

No Eagles or space action and not much in the way of effects or action here. But since this episode is a ghost story, this is not a criticism.

What it lacks in action, the episode makes up for with chills and mood.

The plot is a little slow at times and the logic of the ghost's appearance is a little lacking. How Mateo can be haunted by his own ghost from the future is left unexplained.

But this is a cracker all the same and bound to give a few scares in the right places.

THIS EPISODE:

SPACE BRAIN

SCREENPLAY - CHRISTOPHER PENFOLD

DIRECTED - CHARLES CRICHTON

By all accounts this story probably went through some serious issues behind the scenes as well as some rather funny ones. To suggest it has a reputation which precedes it is not an exaggeration.

But 'Space Brain' is an episode which has much going for it and is often great fun for the fan of pure family-friendly space adventure.

For a start the episode boasts the longest cold open in the series which means by the time we get through the spectacular titles sequence we are about eight minutes in and well involved.

The cold open plays cleverly with the theme of the story too, with various Alphans trying to solve a challenging puzzle. While it happens to be a jigsaw puzzle, the parallel is soon apparent when Alpha is bombarded by weird alien signals and screens full of hieroglyphics and mathematical symbols. Solving a puzzle and trying to communicate is central to the episode and its story.

We're also introduced to the main guest star, Shane Rimmer of *Thunderbirds* fame who gets to develop one of his best performances as Kelly, a stalwart Alphan astronaut who becomes central to the main plot.

Finally, as an Eagle blasts off to investigate the puzzling alien signals, we get a brief taste of Mars, Bringer of War, a classic piece of music from Holst which was famously used in the 1950s as the opening theme of Nigel Kneale's thrilling *Quatermass* serials.

As the strains of Mars crescendo, the Eagle nears a bizarre psychedelic space object, the 'Space Brain', eerie spider web stuff drifts onto the Eagle hull and covers it and contact is lost. Kelly and the ever-ready Alan blast off in a rescue Eagle.

Suddenly a meteorite whizzes past, striking the Moon near outer Alpha, its surface covered in creepy web like strands!

Shane Rimmer does a very good job as Kelly and once again Nick Tate shines as the ever-dependable Alan, who disobeys orders to go into space and rescue his pal Kelly who is falling into a trance out there, exposed to the 'Space Brain's influence.

Apparently, Rimmer and Tate had a fight scene inside the Eagle, but this ended up on the cutting room floor, but back on Alpha, Kelly falls under the control of the Brain and causes more trouble in a manner reminiscent of Helena's behaviour in 'Ring Around the Moon', notably the very fast typing on the computer controls.

When an Eagle loaded up with nukes is sent to blow up the 'Space Brain', Koenig has doubts it is the right course of action.

Koenig decides to find out what is up with Kelly and the Brain by linking his mind electronically to Kelly.

This electronic symbiosis is a nifty idea and allows for some clever visual montages and a fine bit of acting from Martin Landau as he evokes the idea that the Brain is a vast organizing force which sits at the heart of a galaxy filled with innumerable worlds and exotic life forms.

Once it's over, Koenig and Kelly seem to come onto the same page, working with the 'Space Brain', which they now realise is friendly.

Koenig orders the nuke-filled Eagle to be brought back from its attack mission, but there is a fault aboard the ship. The Eagle becomes a flying bomb, aimed at Main Mission.

Koenig takes off, displaying his heroic astronaut skills, docking his Eagle onto the remote-controlled one with its nukes. He disarms the bombs but cannot alter the course of the Eagle with the power of his own ship.

Suspense builds as he plunges toward the moon. At the last moment, he breaks free and the remote-controlled Eagle crashes. What follows is one of *Space:1999*'s most derided sequences, referred to on one DVD release as "there's no place like foam", but this reputation is unjust.

The production team flood the moon base with foam for the climax in which the moon passes through the 'Space Brain', to represent the antibodies of the 'Space Brain' attacking Alpha, but it's intercut with much great FX and action, giving the impression that Alpha is weathering a kind of galactic storm.

The Alphans fight for the survival of their base and one memorable model shot depicts an Eagle being covered by masses of white foam.

The whole climax of the episode is accompanied by the rousing music of Mars, Bringer of War, which is fitting as the Eagle swallowed by foam is reminiscent of the *Quatermass* 2 rocket being covered by alien tendrils in the finale of that serial.

Once again, Christopher Penfold demonstrates his ability to write a lengthy, sustained sequence in which there is much action and peril.

When it's all over, Alpha survives but the 'Space Brain' has perished and Helena laments "if only we could have communicated." This final line brings home the theme of the episode and it is a worthy one.

This, together with Shane Rimmer's presence and the great use of Mars, Bringer of War, help make this a fun and worthy episode. Amazingly, antibody proteins do actually foam and bubble up when exposed to air, making the use of foam a reasonable production choice for the story. A harmless bit of fun to watch with the kids.

COMPUTER'S OBJECTIVE ASSESSMENT

OVERALL PRODUCTION QUALITY

7/10

'Space Brain' is probably a little bit below par in some respects and in some ways feels like it is aimed at a younger audience than many of the other episodes in the series.

Casual viewers will probably find it funny that Moon base Alpha gets deluged in what looks like washing machine foam while Eagles are swamped with shaving cream.

But whatever it is flaws, the episode is lively, colourful and lots of fun.

For most fans it probably brings back happy memories.

THIS EPISODE:

THE INFERNAL MACHINE

SCREENPLAY - ANTHONY TERPILOFF
&
ELIZABETH BARROWS

DIRECTED - DAVID TOMBLIN

A strange ship comes to the Moon, containing an old man called Companion and an unseen presence known as Gwent. When John, Helen and Victor go inside the ship, they learn they are trapped inside a thinking, talking, ruthless machine from a distant planet.

'The Infernal Machine' is a splendid episode with the charming personality of Gwent as played by the wonderful Leo McKern stamped all over it. It's a simple plot but boasts a strong script and production quality and focuses so effectively upon John, Helena, and Victor that it would make a superb introduction episode to the series.

Arguably it should have been screened very early to help viewers connect with the regulars in a strong and engaging way because it may have helped the series find its audience. Koenig gets to be cunning, strong, and ultimately sensitive while Bergman is wise, and Helena gets to play doctor both to Companion and Bergman.

Paul was written out due to actor Prentis Hancock needing a small medical procedure, but Alan gets to be his dependable, heroic self as always. But Gwent and Companion, both played by McKern, are what dominates. 'Infernal Machine' is the tale of a man who put his personality into a colossal and powerful space travelling machine and it outgrows him and finally outlives him. Companion seems amiable enough, but Gwent seem to be gradually becoming corrupted by his own enormous power. In a way, this is a modern take on Dr Jeckyl and Mr Hyde.

The surreal set for the interior of Gwent, where much of the episode takes place, with its strange shapes and vast spaces, the ominous disembodied voice, and the fact the three lead characters are held prisoner inside the machine makes McKern perfect casting since he was Number 2 on two episodes of Patrick McGoohan's surreal classic series *The Prisoner*.

McKern is fun as the aged and forgetful Companion, but ominous as Gwent, the worst part of him, as he calls it, which he leaves behind. Companion dies, his alter ego Gwent lives on, distressed, mourning him, seeking new company, now a megalomaniac in machine form, with no restraints.

Gwent in fact starts to talk and act like a kind of cruel and callous God, enslaving his human captives to help him, his booming voice even saying *Gwent giveth and Gwent taketh away*.

The episode also features a couple of spectacular battle sequences with the machine Gwent blasting Eagles with laser bolts, and Alpha hits back with some very nifty laser tanks. I can only assume these nifty creations were in storage on Alpha and they are finally busted out to take on Gwent.

They seem to be a development of the lunar tanks which appeared in the later episodes of *UFO* but these ones discharge very cool purple laser blasts.

These battle sequences are real highlights of the episode, very well shot and edited, with the stylish explosions and beams that would soon be seen on the big screen in the first *Star Wars* movie.

Another highlight is a scene in which Koenig deduces that Gwent is blind and begins to communicate to Bergman and then to Alpha by writing. His written command to attack is suspenseful and exciting in the way it is presented.

Gwent ends his visit to the Moon with an act of suicide after Koenig stands up to his bullying and Bergman makes him realise the folly of his existence.

Gwent, the machine, is really just a mechanised abomination which exists purely as a monument to one man's ego.

When Bergman points out how wrong this is, to be motivated by pride and vanity, trying to preserve one's personality, Gwent seems to have an awakening and realisation. It's top-notch writing and the cast deliver it with skill and resonance.

All in all, this is one of *Space: 1999*'s finest episodes and holds a level of broad appeal which few other episodes can match. If it has any flaws, they are probably simply down to the fact that things move at a slow pace, occasionally, compared to modern standards.

But a few slow stretches aside, 'The Infernal Machine' remains a charming, engaging, and impressive production which stands up as one of *Space:1999*'s best.

COMPUTER'S OBJECTIVE ASSESSMENT

OVERALL PRODUCTION QUALITY

9/10

'Infernal Machine' is a classy episode and although the three main characters to spend an awfully long time standing around on one set arguing with a disembodied voice it somehow manages to feel like a very high-quality piece of writing and acting.

The episode probably could have done with a little more action, but the space battle sequences which feature are spectacular and very well done with exploding ships which look like something out of *Star Wars*.

A very good quality episode, only let down by a few slow patches here and there.

The ending is very touching and well done.

THIS EPISODE:

MISSION OF THE DARIANS

SCREENPLAY - JOHNNY BYRNE

DIRECTED - RAY AUSTIN

This episode has perhaps the greatest scale of any story in the series, because it is set aboard a colossal alien spaceship with a vast and multifaceted interior, a virtual city in space.

The episode features a cold open which is very much like a precursor to the scene in the first *Star Wars* movie in which Han Solo's ship is pulled into the Death Star by an invisible tractor beam. Responding to a distress signal from space, the Alphans set off to investigate a colossal drifting star ship, are captured by an invisible beam and pulled in, Koenig wondering if they can ever get back out again.

Perhaps it is more than coincidence that Han Solo and friends think the Death Star is a "moon" when they first see it in space?

Perhaps the most remarkable thing about the episode 'Mission of the Darians' is the fact that the plight of the crew of the gigantic alien spaceship mirrors the plight of the humans on Moonbase.

The parallels between the situations of the first people and the alien people they meet in this episode of very thought provoking. The leader of the Darians has set himself up as a kind of God-figure to control his people who have degenerated into barbarism and suffered a number of mutations.

This part of the plot may not seem to mirror anything about Alpha on the face of it, but the possibility is certainly there that Alpha could go this way in the future. Koenig was accused of *playing God* by Bergman in his dream sequence in the surreal 'Missing Link' episode and certainly it was Koenig who decided the fate of the Alphans when he announced they would not be attempting a return to Earth after the 'Breakaway' event sent them out of orbit.

The idea that the leader has the potential to become a manipulator and maybe even a kind of megalomaniac in the fight for survival, that he might adopt a God-like role over his people in some perverse and twisted way, is an interesting one.

The suggestion that the Alphans, like the Darians, could end up living in a destroyed and drifting hulk, which was once their base, degenerating and possibly mutating from radioactive contamination, returning to semi barbarism, is also fascinating to consider.

The crew of the drifting and helpless generation starship are concealing a very dark secret, too.

After the humans go board and explore the ship and meet various characters they eventually discover the grisly truth. It seems the only way for the crew to survive is through cannibalism. Mutated survivors of the space disaster which crippled the ship back in the past are being killed and harvested as a food saw supply.

There is also some notion of harvesting organs to extend life for the Darian leaders, an idea which seems to harken back to the premise of the Andersons' *UFO* series, where aliens were taking human organs to extend their existences.

Joan Collins makes a striking guest appearance in the episode, although not quite as strong as her memorable role on *Star Trek*'s 'City on the Edge of Forever' episode. Here, she is forced to admit the moral degradation of her people and at the end, Koenig plays mediator, forcing her character to face the leader of the barbarians she and her kind were preying upon and manipulating.

Alan Carter and Paul Morrow get some great scenes here, with Alan overpowering and exposing a so-called God and forcing him to admit to being just a man in a silver suit and helmet. Alan leads the revolution, too.

The episode features amazing matte painting shots to emphasise the vastness of the Darian ship and the inhabitants even include some dwarf actors who turn in very good performances.

Science Fiction has always been about creating a greater appreciation for diversity and the show certainly captures a sense of a very mixed assortment of people who must learn to set their conflicts aside and work together for a better future in the end.

At the end of the episode Alan asks John Koenig what he would decide to do it the same situation which happened on the Darian ship were to occur on their Moon Base.

Although the Commander avoids answering the question in a rather light-hearted manner, the fact the question remains unanswered is haunting and disturbing because we've just seen it dramatized.

The episode makes it clear to us that the people of Moon Base Alpha have been lucky so far to avoid the worst possible scenarios connected with their situation, the worst possible consequences.

Although lost in space at the mercy of a dangerous universe, the humans have not been forced to make the worst decisions and face a truly grizzly fight for final survival. At least, not yet.

It's a very dark idea and the episode is very brave for putting it forward. The way the concept is pitched is reminiscent of the science fiction film *Soylent Green* in which the bodies of the dead are turned into food to sustain life for the people of an overpopulated future world.

Soylent Green was adapted from a novel called *Make Room, Make Room,* which dealt with overpopulation. The notion that Alpha's population could become unsustainable some day in the future is a scary one and seems to be the case for the Darians.

With the passing of time and Earth's own population growing rapidly, the story is more relevant today than it was when the series was made.

Powerful viewing, cloaked in a space adventure tale, 'Mission of the Darians' gives us food for thought, but not an easy theme to stomach!

COMPUTER'S OBJECTIVE ASSESSMENT

OVERALL PRODUCTION QUALITY

9/10

Huge in scale and spectacular for its time, this is a sprawling space epic.

The downside is that the story unfolds a little slowly at times and some of the horror of the theme is more disturbing than exciting.

All in all, though, this is one of the series most impressive productions and while it lacks action, it's definitely well worth watching.

THIS EPISODE

DRAGON'S DOMAIN

SCREENPLAY - CHRISTOPHER PENFOLD

DIRECTED - CHARLES CRICHTON

When *Space: 1999* premiered in the United States, actors Martin Landau and Barbara Bain appeared on US television to introduce their show to American viewers. They gave the viewers a classy introduction, including mentioning of how far we had come since Armstrong's first steps on the Moon and referenced the international space project in which the Russians and Americans had done a space link up, something very recent at the time of broadcast.

At the end of 'Breakaway's screening, they previewed the next episode. The preview which was shown was for 'Dragon's Domain'. The decision to screen this as episode two in the series was a very good one because it is one of the best episodes of the entire series if not the absolute best hands down. It was something similar to what had happened with the debut of *Star Trek* in the 60s, where the salt-vampire episode was shown early to get audiences hooked in with a monster.

'Dragon's Domain' begins with an intriguing teaser about an Alphan called Tony Cellini who is haunted by nightmares about a monster and one of the interesting things which makes the episode stand apart from many others in the series is that Dr Helena Russell narrates much of the episode.

This includes introducing Tony and his mortal enemy, which is initially unclear.

We immediately see that Tony's living quarters is adorned with weapons and images associated with hunting, which says much about his character. This is the most mythic episode of *Space: 1999* of them all, for it deals with a storyline very much like the legend of Beowulf, the dragon slayer, and it also compares Tony directly to *Saint George and the Dragon*.

Tony tries to hijack an Eagle ship, attacking the hapless Alan Carter along the way, only to be shot down with a stun blast by Koenig seconds later. We soon learn that Koenig and Cellini are old friends, and that Koenig has great admiration for the man.

In a flashback sequence we learn a lot of information about the backstory of Commander Koenig, Professor Bergman, and Dr Russell, our three main regular characters, and we also meet another Commissioner who preceded Commissioner Simmonds.

There is some questionable astronomy in this story, which is typical of the episodes by writer, Christopher Penfold, because the episode suggests that an Earth-type planet has been discovered just beyond the fringes of our solar system and can be reached by an Earth space probe.

If we take a forgiving approach, we might assume that the planet called Ultra has arrived near our system through one of the many wormholes or space time windows which appear to permeate the Universe in this series, the same time warps and wormholes which allow the drifting Moon itself to jump light years across the galaxy at times.

But leaving this notion aside, or simply accepting that astronomy is not Penfold's strength as a writer, we can focus instead on Penfold's ability to construct a gripping narrative and give us vivid, unforgettable imagery, something we will also see in 'War Games'.

The plot of 'Dragon's Domain' unfolds swiftly and gracefully with some very well-chosen classical music accompaniment and Dr Russell's narration to bridge shifts and add salient details. This sequence is exceptionally effective, allowing us to go with Tony Cellini and his crew aboard the Ultra space probe as it heads out on its mission beyond the limits of the solar system. Soon the months have passed, and the probe has encountered a graveyard of drifting spaceships of all shapes and sizes, an ominous sight.

The probe ship docks onto one of the drifting craft and the crew wait for a chance to board, as Tony stays in the cockpit. Finally, the doors open...

In the single most relentless and well sustained piece of horror ever to appear in *Space: 1999*, a roaring, one eyed monster with long, thick brown tentacles like those of an octopus or squid, simply appears, or materializes, in the open hatchway of the Ultra probe ship. Its single eye emits a bright white light which seems to exert a hypnotic effect upon the crew members, enrapturing them perhaps, rather like the Sirens of ancient Greek mythology which could lure sea travellers to their deaths. This rapture the creature exerts seems to last until its tentacles can take hold of their bodies, curling around their limbs and even throats, catching them like fish.

One after another, Tony Cellini's entire crew is dragged by the tentacles into the open mouth of the monster, screaming and begging with such cries as, "don't hurt me!"

It consumes them completely, then spits out their steaming, flesh-less skeletons. Trapped in the cockpit by a sudden malfunction, Tony is unable to help. Finally, he gets the door open and confronts the monster, just seconds too late to save anyone.

The beast proves to be immune to laser fire, too, as Tony blasts away at it, before being forced to flee as it tries to grab him. The monster attempts to use its hypnotic thrall upon him and Tony only manages to survive by fighting off its probing tentacles with a fire axe. He seals himself back in the cockpit, separates the nose cone of the probe and flees back to Moon base. It's a long journey to make alone in a cramped nose cone, but he makes it to Alpha, arriving barely alive.

We get one of the most interesting sequences in *Space:1999* when Koenig and Bergman are called into Commissioner Dixon's office for an inquiry into the Ultra probe case, along with the recovered Tony. Here we learn who Koenig is at heart. He is a man driven by a passion for space exploration and pursuit of knowledge about the Universe, a drive to help Mankind cross the frontiers to the stars. Like Alan Carter, he is an astronaut of top rank, and this explains both the admiration Alan shows him, particularly when he displays "a nice bit of flying" in the 'Space Brain' episode and Koenig's continual insistence on being hands-on when it comes to flying Eagles, getting out into space.

In this inquiry, we also see Koenig's passionate and fiery defence of Tony Cellini, which is also a sign of his loyalty to his friends, another key aspect of Koenig's character. He fights for those he cares for, and we see this clearly when he defends Tony against accusations of insanity or neglect.

We also see that, when his beliefs are at stake, he has an antagonistic relationship with authority. 'Dragon's Domain', like 'Breakaway' and 'Earthbound', bring Koenig into conflict with a Commissioner with strong, dramatic results. Commander Straker on *UFO* had clashed with his superior, General Henderson, on many occasions and it's telling that the three *Space:1999* episodes in which Koenig rebels against a Commissioner are among the series most compelling. But leaping to Cellini's defence and arguing for more space exploration gets Koenig grounded by Dixon.

This is something which clearly was reversed by Simmonds when the Commission needed the Meta Probe launched. Clearly, they saw in Koenig a man with the fire in his spirit necessary to get the mission underway as it became mired in the virus infection drama. It is this same drive, the same fire, that makes Koenig the strong leader now that Alpha is lost in the void.

After Helena's voice over covers the 'Breakaway', the narrative comes back to the present moment as Tony recovers from his attempted hijacking of an Eagle and tells the Commander and the doctor that he was going out into space to face his monster. This hints that Cellini has somehow managed to almost sense the presence of his monster on a psychic or subconscious level is something which will happen time and again in the series.

Sure enough, Alpha appears to be approaching the same graveyard of spaceships which contains the abandoned Ultra probe ship.

In the gripping climax the Alphans, including Tony, come face-to-face with the monster once again. Tony has clearly had many years to think about the monster and its immunity to lasers and he races ahead to get to the monster first, even stealing an Eagle to do so. Poor Alan cops another blow, allowing Nick Tate to charm us further with his reactions. But the showdown with the monster has the viewer on edge, much like the scenes in a Hitchcock thriller where someone heads into the lair of a killer.

Docking the nosecone of his stolen Eagle on the abandoned Ultra probe ship, Cellini is able to get inside, to face his foe. He uses a rope and grapple hook to prevent the monster from pulling him into its open mouth when it appears and he begins to launch his own ferocious attack upon it with a knife, stabbing it repeatedly until it bleeds, venting his years of anger perhaps or finally striking avenging blows for the deaths of his crew members.

But one of its tentacles wraps around his rope, even as he stabs the monster and as the rope splits and finally breaks, Tony is pulled into the mouth of his monster and dies, having inflicted mortal wounds upon the creature. Koenig and Dr Russell arrive in time to see the truth of Tony's story about the monster but moments too late to save him.

Koenig quickly realizes lasers and blasters have no effect and uses Tony's fallen Tomahawk instead to attack the monster. As Koenig repeatedly strikes the eye of the monster with the axe, the creature finally succumbs to its wounds and dies.

'Dragon's Domain' is quite simply one of the most gripping, suspenseful, harrowing hours of science-fiction horror ever broadcast. It is rich in background information about the characters and the monster itself is superbly done. It plays out like

Alien before *Alien* was made and no doubt sent
many 70s children to bed feeling afraid to sleep
with the lights out because, in short, it is the stuff of
nightmares.

COMPUTER'S OBJECTIVE ASSESSMENT

OVERALL PRODUCTION QUALITY

10/10

'Dragon's Domain' is undoubtedly the best episode of the entire series.

Stagehands using wires bring the rubber tentacles and glowing eye of the alien monster to life in a way that is startling and convincing.

The horror, suspense and drama are all first rate, and the guest cast are excellent. It is a mythic epic and a story that can be enjoyed by the fan and the casual viewer alike.

See it and love it, for it is truly outstanding.

THIS EPISODE:

TESTAMENT OF ARKADIA

SCREENPLAY - JOHNNY BYRNE

DIRECTED - DAVID TOMBLIN

With this episode, one of television's greatest accomplishments comes to an end, and it is no small thing.

This is the third time the series addresses the notion of an invisible, intelligent force influencing the moon's odyssey and this time, there seems to be hard evidence to support the theories and elaborate claims of the earlier episodes.

This then, is the moment Koenig's beliefs about the fate of Alpha shift from believing their journey is a random accident to a kind of faith, a faith in a purpose for Alpha and for all of Mankind.

And that's *Space:1999* in a nutshell, a journey from a belief that life and the Universe are random to a kind of faith that the Universe is intelligent and contains wisdom and that life has a purpose.

The story begins when Alpha and the moon are brought to a dead stop in space by an unseen force and Alpha begins to lose power. The Alphans head for a nearby planet, Arkadia, seeking answers.

Once there, they find a cave containing a message from people who died long ago. It's written in the Earth language Sanskrit and seems to reveal that these people, having destroyed their world in a nuclear war, went into space to find a new home and the planet they found was Earth.

Two Alphans, Luke and Anna, cause a lot of trouble until they are allowed to stay on the planet as a new Adam and Eve, to return human life to its place of origin. With this requirement fulfilled, the moon is set free again to continue on its journey, the power coming back to full.

Koenig seems to see this experience as confirming the things theorised by Bergman in 'Black Sun' and told to him by Arra in 'Collision Course', because he concludes *we must keep faith and believe that for us, for all Mankind, there is a purpose.*

One of the questions some viewers have raised over the years about 'Testament of Arkadia' are about the real possibility of Alphans Luke and Anna repopulating the planet in the manner of Adam and Eve. Whatever the factual details of such a situation, it is probably largely irrelevant.

The real point of the situation is that the story is symbolic, it should be taken somewhat poetically, viewed with some allowance for artistic license. Why? Simply because it is a space age re-enactment of the story of Adam and Eve, a mythical story line and it serves to make a point about Mankind's destiny among the stars.

Some critics have attacked the episode over the years as a Shaggy God story, the type of cliched sci fi short story that ends with a pair of astronauts turning out to be Adam and Eve after crash-landing on a planet conspicuously endowed with apple trees and the odd snake. Certainly, this type of story had been done on *Twilight Zone* and was a hoary old cliché.

But in the context of *Space: 1999*'s epic season one, it's the perfect ending to the central myth arc which began in 'Black Sun' and was developed in 'Collision Course'.

By returning human life to Arkadia, the place of Humanity's origin, the Alphans have fulfilled a purpose and proven that their journey has not simply been a series of random, meaningless accidents and experiences. It's also pertinent to note that the testament itself speaks of Arkadia flaming in the heat of a thousand suns, as if the Arkadians destroyed themselves in a nuclear war.

The anti-nuclear theme here ties back well to the anti-war theme of 'War Games' and its notions that humans carry the seed of their own destruction. Taking the seeds of life to the stars and finding a new world and a fresh start is an idea which ties back to the original episode when the event of the 'Breakaway' seemed to confirm in dramatic terms that Armstrong's conquest of the moon was indeed the beginning of Mankind setting off to find its true destiny out among the stars.

'Black Sun', 'Collision Course' and 'Testament of Arkadia' are the spiritual core of *Space:1999* and the lesson Koenig takes away, that there is a purpose to it all, is the perfect way to end the season. The fact the whole episode is narrated by Koenig who is writing about the events on the planet gives the whole thing the feeling of a story in a book, possibly only as accurate as the memories of the person telling the tale. The episode concludes, and the series closes on Koenig closing the journal he's been writing in and laying down his pen. In a way, it helps frame the storyline and perhaps even the series as something of mythic story, albeit told in a space setting.

This is a terrific episode to end the series on, an episode which confirms that there is much more to this series than just a random set of adventures for a drifting moon. 'Testament of Arkadia' underlines everything which makes *Space:1999* an absolutely unique series, a work of art which has rarely been matched or attempted again.

And it reminds us that these 24 episodes have been an experience to savour and celebrate.

COMPUTER'S OBJECTIVE ASSESSMENT

OVERALL PRODUCTION QUALITY

9/10

'Testament of Arcadia' is the perfect ending to the series. There is no great action content and special effects are kept to a minimum. However, despite feeling a little bit barebones at times episode has an epic and majestic feeling.

The revelation about Man's origins in space make a brilliant final twist for the series. The fact that Koenig and the Alphans as a whole have survived their odyssey, despite their human vulnerability and fallibility seems due to faith. While Simmonds fell apart and met his doom in 'Earthbound', Koenig's increasing faith in humanity and something greater than himself has gotten them through the trials of their journey.

Koenig gaining of faith is a nice complement to the Bible parallel of the Adam and Eve plotline.

All in all a meaningful episode and a very fine and commendable ending to an outstanding series.

Space: 1999

Year Two

AUTHOR'S NOTE

It might seem like a funny thing to say at the start of a book, but this is something I feel needs to be said because *Space:1999's* second year has been a traditionally controversial series, even with *Space:1999*'s most devoted fans.

So, I want to make this clear as I sit down to write. Obviously, I am writing this book for people who like season two. Writing a book for people who hate it would be silly and pointless, in my opinion, something I am not interested in doing.

Anyone can be a naysayer and add fuel to the fires of negativity but that's just not going to lead to an insightful or valuable read, in my view. So, this book will be as positive as possible, while hopefully not forgetting to be accurate as well.

Science fiction series often become divisive in the eyes of their fans. There are people who are fans of the BBC's *Doctor Who*, for example, but they hate the 80s era of John Nathan Turner, or they hate the modern revival which began in 2005. There are fans of the original iterations of *Star Trek* and *Star Wars* who take exception to the later revivals of those classics, too.

But there are also those who find something to enjoy in all eras of their favourite shows and series and this book is for those who want to find the good in *Space:1999*'s second season. If you want to know what's good in *Space:1999* year two, I hope this book will help you find it and enjoy it just that little bit more.

To me, season two of *Space:1999* is simply like a different, and later, era of *Space:1999*, somewhat removed from the first, it seems, but still the same show and still containing much to enjoy, even if it's not quite as awesome as it used to be. I think this fact needs to be made clear from the outset.

If you're a strictly year one fan of *Space:1999*, then this book of year two episodes is probably not intended for you. Although, if you're open-minded enough to consider the idea that maybe there are new things to learn about year two, then maybe it is. If you are open to the idea that year two could have more going for it than you had previously noticed, I hope this book will be a good read for you.

Season one of *Space:1999* was amazing television, no question about that. It had brilliant production values which seemed next level for TV at the time and an atmosphere that could chill the blood and frighten our inner child!

I remember the arrival of year one on my local screens vividly. It was exciting and there was a lot of buzz which followed because in Australia, we were used by ITC as a test market for *Space: 1999*.

We were inundated with marketing and promotion, including competitions, swap cards,

168

toys, even a visit by a tour bus with people dressed as Alphans in it. Year one landed, in my home country, with an amazing impact. I couldn't walk down a street without kids approaching from across the road because they had spotted my collection of *Space:1999* swap cards in my hands and wanted to see if I had anything to trade with them.

But year two was treated far less well by local broadcasters. It just began to air one Saturday afternoon and I seem to recall they not only failed to promote it, but they didn't even start with the 'Metamorph' episode, skipping it for something more time slot appropriate. I don't recall ever seeing a TV promo for a year two episode in Australia.

But despite the shabby way it was treated in terms of programming and time slots, and the critical flak it received from many quarters, year two still managed to win me over. In fact, I was devoted to the point of hunting the episodes all over the schedule and being sure to catch it no matter when it was airing.

While set sometime later than year one and featuring many changes, the season is still worth watching and often very enjoyable on its own merits, in my view.

In this book, I want to talk about the episodes and stories, the characters and the highlights of this fabulous show's controversial second season, as well as the underlying changes which took place.

And for that, it will be necessary to take a trip back in time, to see where the story really begins.

It will be necessary to take a trip to Moon Base Alpha, too, in search of meaning and understanding.

So, with that said, strap yourself in, fellow Alphan. Eagle One is ready for lift off, it's time to fly into the vast uncharted dimensions of hyperspace, hop a handy space-time warp back to the mid-1970s and discover what's out there.

PROLOGUE:
THE METAMORPHOSIS OF A TELEVISION SERIES

In the later part of the Second World War, a short Jewish American pilot finds himself in the same German Prisoner of War camp where the famous movie *The Great Escape* would someday be set. It is a place of barbed wire, mud, bleakness, and brutality, under the iron rule of the Nazi regime.

Being of Jewish descent, the young P.O.W named Fred Freiberger would find himself in a very tough predicament for a period of two years before freedom finally beckoned.

Despite the infamous brutality of the Germans, Freiberger would eventually return home to the United States, safe and sound, where he would go on to work in television production and earn a reputation as a likeable and amiable man, someone who would become an important figure in television science fiction in the 1960s and 70s.

But, despite his good-natured personality and his undeniable success, Frieberger would eventually become a figure of deeply entrenched controversy in the eyes of science fiction fans.

First, this would come as a result of his time as producer of Gene Roddenberry's *Star Trek*. Next, it would be doubled down upon by many hard-core fans of Gerry and Sylvia Anderson's *Space:1999*.

171

Quarter of a century after his time on *Star Trek*, he would lament that the Germans had only tormented him for two years, his suffering at the hands of Trek fans had lasted 25 years and counting. Doubtless, many *Space:1999* fans gave him just as much ire. Dubbed the 'serial killer', he would get everything from his TV work except popularity and respect.

Yet, despite this unhappy fact, Freiberger has, to this day, his defenders who claim he is not the "show killer" or "series killer" of TV legend, or infamy, but a much more sympathetic figure, a man who deserves a re-evaluation.

Space:1999 was a surprisingly popular series when it first aired on television in the mid-1970s, particularly in the all-important US market. Ratings were high, the money from sales to the US market proved good and Lew Grade's investment seemed to pay off with a hit, even without the series being taken up by one of the networks.

But despite this, there was little chance of the series continuing. Like most series made by independent television in those days, it was faced with the likelihood of financier Lord Lew Grade simply moving on to a new project, hoping as ever to find the next big thing.

The same fate had befallen *UFO*, its second season being transformed into *Space:1999*. This was bad news for fans of *UFO* and for its cast, but Grade was right that a new show would get a better chance in the international market. It seemed likely that *Space:1999* would also be cancelled after one season and the team behind it would move on to a new idea.

But as fate would have it, *Space:1999* did manage to get the green light for a second season. However, the green light came only after considerable effort was made to transform the series into something which could promise to offer a new direction on the one hand, and which could be produced on a lower budget at the same time.

At the end of the *Space:1999* season one wrap party, Gerry Anderson announced, for reasons presumably known only to himself, to the cast and crew of the series, that he and *Space:1999* Producer Sylvia Anderson, would be divorcing. This meant the end of not only their marriage but their professional relationship as well, and Sylvia departed her role on *Space:1999*.

Her legacy was considerable, because *Space:1999* had been a remarkable series and its spectacular production values had left a lasting impact on a generation of television viewers around the globe.

To replace her was no mean feat and it is perhaps a little curious that the replacement would eventually be Fred Freiberger, producer of the third and final season of *Star Trek*.

Working with Gerry Anderson, Freiberger would change *Space:1999* into a series which, at face value, seemed almost like a whole new show. But despite this transformation and the somewhat alienating effect it sometimes had on viewers, season two is still the same show. It just takes a bit of scrutiny, at times, to really see it.

Season two kicks off in considerable style with the episode 'The Metamorph', by Johnny Byrne, although the word style might be a stretch when it comes to Koenig's new coat, a sort of sleeveless thing added to his regular Alpha uniform which he wisely decides to never wear again in the rest of the season. Presumably someone noticed it didn't look good on camera and it was promptly tossed out.

In previous years, when a costume didn't work on *UFO*, the show whose second season evolved into *Space:1999*, there would've been re-shoots, but here we come to one of the notable things about season two of *Space:1999*. There was no time allowed for re-shoots, at least not to the extent there had been in previous years.

Sylvia Anderson had left the series and there was a new producer in town. His name was Freddie Freiberger, and his new broom was making a clean sweep of what went before.

Under Sylvia Anderson's stewardship, the first season of *1999* had been one of the most meticulously well visualised series ever produced, a lavish feast for the eyes and a thing of rare beauty.

It had, for the period, cost a staggering amount of money. But the budget had not only been devoured by classy production values and attention to visual detail. British film and television production in the 1970s was highly unionised and the unions had firm control over shooting schedules. This meant a major limit on the available time to shoot an episode.

With the arrival of American Freiberger, *1999* was now going to take on this stifling limitation with a set of time saving tactics the Anderson team had never considered before. So, all this begs the question: was Fred Freiberger a terrible producer? And furthermore, did he ruin *Space: 1999*?

Well, the truth is, it's complicated.

WHERE IS EVERYBODY?

Seasons one and two of *Space:1999* are often talked about as being very, very different from each other. Some say season two is almost like a completely different show. Certainly, there are many differences, many changes and the flavour is very different from one to the other.

It seems fair to say that how well we reconcile the differences between season one and season two has a very big impact on our ability to accept and enjoy the second season.

The biggest question for many fans of the first season concerns the absence of characters such as computer operator David Kano, Controller Paul Morrow and most notable of all, Professor Victor Bergman.

Bergman in particular is the loss most keenly felt, it seems. The Professor or Barry Morse's performance in the role, was often compared by British fans and critics to Patrick Troughton's incarnation of the BBC's *Doctor Who*, so for those who loved and adored the character, a season of *Space:1999* without the Professor was, perhaps, like a season of *Doctor Who* with no Doctor. The word disappointment doesn't even begin to cover it.

And it is fair to say neither Gerry Anderson nor Fred Freiberger understood how much Professor Bergman was part of the flavour of *Space:1999* which kept its fans tuning in from week to week.

So, where exactly did these people go?

According to Producer Fred Freiberger, his notion was simple. There are 311 men and women on Moon Base Alpha and the absent crew members are simply lost in the mix, somewhere in the crowd, among all those people.

Taking this notion to its logical conclusion, they are still on Alpha, just reassigned to some other part of the lunar colony, away from the central command and control area.

It is a well-documented fact that the script for one of the early episodes of the second season featured a line, spoken by Tony, which stated that the Professor had died due to a fault in a spacesuit.

However, the production team decided to remove this line of dialogue from the episode. I think it was right to remove this line of dialogue because it would have contradicted the idea that the Professor was simply elsewhere, lost in the mix of the 300 or so people on the moon base.

Since the line was not included in the transmitted episode, I feel we are meant to believe the Professor and the other missing characters are simply elsewhere in the base.

It was strongly suggested in the first season that there was some sort of relationship forming between Paul and Sandra, too, so, although we don't see Paul, it is not unreasonable to suppose he is still on the base and probably involved with Sandra.

In the episode 'The Lambda Factor', it is suggested that the people of the base have relationships and marriages and often move into sharing living quarters with each other. Since the only time we see Sandra with someone romantically in season two is when she appears to be reunited with her lost fiancé from Earth in 'Bringers of Wonder', where her lost love is merely an alien-created illusion of her past, it seems reasonable then to assume she could be sharing her off duty life with Paul, during season two.

Paul may simply be spending his working hours in a different section of the lunar base where we do not see him. He could be coming home from his working days to a living situation with Sandra, but we don't see him as the series generally focuses upon activities which take place in Alpha's central command and control areas.

There are many outer areas it seems, where the missing characters could be working and living, a sprawling ring of the circular colony we might call outer-Alpha.

In the first season, there were certainly many instances of people on the base who appeared for a particular episode and then were either killed off or simply never seen again, even down to people who worked in some sections we only saw once, such as the nuclear generating section or the botanic area.

Benjamin Ouma vanishes after 'Breakaway' for example, with David Kano simply arriving in Main Mission thereafter.

It seems a logical conclusion that people can be reassigned to different parts of the base since it is the size of the city.

If we accept that certain personnel have moved to other areas of the colony and some new faces have simply been given appointments to the central command area of the base, in the gap between year one and year two, then it all makes a kind of sense.

Just the fact that we see about four different male doctors, who act as assistants to Dr Russell, is a good adjunct to this concept.

In a base the size of a city, with over 300 personnel, one would expect several doctors, several scientists, several astronauts, and several experts in other areas as well.

The idea that they could rotate for a period of a year or two between different sections seems quite reasonable and probably good for people's mental and emotional well-being.

It was suggested in the American magazine Starlog that the Alphans had moved underground for the sake of survival, having found themselves vulnerable to alien attack and other dangers in deep space. Since Alpha was cast into the depths of space having never been designed to cope out there, this idea of a change for the sake of survival seems to make sense.

With the retractable pair of laser cannons and the move to the smaller subterranean Command Center it seems the Alphans are more militant in season two and focused on their survival now. It is not unreasonable to suppose that people in their position might go through a more conservative period, in which they become focused on survival at all costs, setting aside the more noble ideals of exploration for the short term.

Does this rule out the idea that they will eventually colonise the farthest reaches of space? I see no reason why it should. In fact, it might increase their chances of making it to their destiny intact.

The Alphans appear to have salvaged weaponry and hardware from alien ships, too. The gun from Dione's ship *Satazius*, in 'The Last Enemy', appears on Alpha in 'The Dorcons' and, in 'Space Warp', we also see the Alphans take and keep the device from the alien derelict ship which enables them to chart a way through a space warp.

In at least three episodes we see the Alphans are mining under the moon and have turned at least one underground cave into a research area.

The move to an underground Command Center seems to be consistent with this idea of the wandering humans burrowing under the moon as they attempt to expand and consolidate their colony. It might've been fascinating to see a third season where Alpha was now decked out with alien weaponry and other salvaged tech and the Alphans were now living largely under the surface, perhaps with several aliens having joined the crew in the same way Maya does.

From the optimism of 'Alpha Child', to the statement in 'The Exiles' that they can no longer allow any more births on Alpha due to limited resources, it seems the plight of our heroes has become considerably tougher by the time of season two and our heroes are now toughening up to face what is out there.

One interesting point is that our heroes wear jackets with their uniforms in almost every instance in the second season. In the first season, they only wore jackets when there was a power loss and the base was getting colder, such as in the episode 'Testament of Arkadia'.

This makes me wonder if the base is operating with less power in season two and therefore the environment could be colder. Perhaps the Alphans now all wear jackets because it uses less energy to keep warm than relying on the base heating system.

For the wandering Earthlings of Moon Base Alpha, the way ahead seems dark and bleak, despite some added colour. But as always, there is plenty of reason to hope.

THE METAMORPH

The Moon approaches the planet Psychon, and hopes are raised that this planet could be a source of titanium, which is needed to repair Alpha's life support system at this point in the base's wayward cosmic journey.

A survey Eagle piloted by Bill Fraser and co-pilot Torrens heads down to take a look at the planet. It's a fiery world of active volcanoes and the surface is uninhabitable.

However, a mysterious ball of green light appears and chases the Eagle through space, engulfing it. At first it appears they have been destroyed, but they are actually the unwilling guests of the alien Mentor and his mysterious daughter Maya, who live deep below the planet's volcanic and turbulent surface.

Mentor contacts Alpha, claiming to be friendly and invites Koenig to visit. But when Koenig, Alan and Helena venture to the planet in an Eagle, it turns out to be a trap.

Mentor's dark secret is a plan to restore his now turbulent and volcanic planet back to the beautiful world it once was. But to this end, he needs to drain mental energy from the brains of all visitors from space who come to Psychon, This energy is for Psyche, a vast biological computer. Once it has enough mental power stored in it, Psyche can transform Psychon completely.

Mentor tries to coerce Koenig into ordering Operation Exodus and bringing the Alphans down to the planet so their minds can be drained by Psyche. Koenig attempts a ploy, pretending to give up but sending a coded message to Alpha, requesting that a robot Eagle be sent to bomb Psychon.

When the plan fails, Mentor goes on the attack. It is Mentor's daughter, Maya, who saves the day. She has the power of molecular transformation and Koenig convinces her to investigate the truth about her father. When she finds out what he is doing, she frees the Alpha party.

Koenig destroys the Psyche computer, but its power causes the whole planet to break up. Mentor is trapped by fire and pleads with Maya to understand he had good intentions.

Koenig and Helena take Maya into their Eagle. They narrowly escape the explosive destruction of Psychon and Maya, now the last of her species, is welcomed to join the crew of Moon Base Alpha.

'The Metamorph' is a generally exciting and entertaining episode. The guest characters of Mentor and his daughter Maya are played by actors well-known to fans of the first season of *Space: 1999*. Brian Blessed, who was superb as the misguided scientist Dr Rowland in 'Death's Other Dominion', returns to help launch *Space:1999*'s second year and he is very good in his role as Maya's father.

He is well known these days as a very loud actor who is famous for his shouting and over-the-top performances. This is largely due to his performance in the movie *Flash Gordon*, where he played the King of the Hawk Men and delivered the line "Gordon's Alive".

However, he is also an accomplished serious actor, with a long and prestigious career. For example, he appears in the 1990s movie *Henry V*, starring Kenneth Brannagh. In the role of Mentor, he is commanding and compelling, just charming enough to avoid being a melodramatic villain.

Although he is clearly ruthless, he is also clearly another misguided scientist who wants to save his world and his people and is quite genuine about this. The fact that he is prepared to go to terrible lengths in order to achieve this goal is shocking, but he is a good man doing bad things, rather than just a B movie villain.

Maya makes a very strong debut here, too. Catherine Schell is immediately likeable as the cheeky and playful shape-changer.

She seems somewhat naive and is clearly oblivious to the true nature of her father's actions.

Martin Landau also turns in a strong performance.

One of the interesting things here is that Alan Carter is clearly a late addition to the script. He probably should have seen through the Commander's ruse when ordering the destruction of the planet, but he doesn't.

Considering the Commander pulled a similar act in the first season episode 'The Last Enemy', pretending to run out on Alpha, it should be fairly obvious by now to Alan that when the Commander appears to betray the Alphans and sell them out to Mentor that's just an act.

The way Alan reacts makes me wonder if his part in the script was originally written for some other member of the Alpha crew.

It's possible that the lines and actions we were given to Alan at a late stage.

Tony Verdeschi does not have a particularly impressive debut in this episode but does reasonably well in the scenes where he orders the attack on the planet in response to the Commander's coded directive.

There is a feeling that the episode is trying hard to deliver a very clear plotline which viewers can easily follow in response to critical condemnation of some of the more bizarre and unfathomable plot twists in some season one episodes. Some early moments are so spelled out as to seem a little patronising.

There is also a feeling here that the writer is trying to suggest a much more emotional and humanised crew than was obvious to critics and casual viewers in the first season.

For example, Bill Fraser has a wife in this episode, and she faints when he appears to have been killed early on. This is reminiscent of the way Sandra passed out when Mike Ryan was killed in his Eagle in the season one episode 'Black Sun'. However, Bill is not dead and so we get a happy reunion later on, perhaps indicating that happy endings are now part of the show's new direction, too.

But before the happy reunion we also have wife Annie's near hysterical response when Tony orders the robot Eagle to destroy the planet where Bill and the Commander and the rest are being held prisoner.

Zienia Merton was particularly pleased that it was Annie who fainted this time around and not her again.

Martin Landau excels in the scenes where he is forced to order the destruction of himself and the others on the planet. Special mention should also go to the role of Torens. Although he has no dialogue, actor Nick Brimble gives 100% to his performance when he is strapped down and has his mind drained into Mentor's evil machine.

In production terms, the debut episode of season two looks expensive and impressive. Brian Johnson's visual effects are, if anything, even better than the visual effects he often delivered for the first season. The occasional use of cardboard cutouts of Eagles for some effect shots in season one episodes like 'War Games' and 'Missing Link' are a thing of the past, now.

Johnson gives us miniature shots of the surface of planet Psychon in which volcanoes erupt, spewing lava, flame and smoke. In the finale of the episode, he gives us an Eagle taking off from an exploding planet.

The planet surface has a graveyard of ships, too, and the explosion of the planet at the very end is very spectacular. The balls of light and Eagles being chased or pulled down are also very well realised by the effect department, with close ups of booster engines pouring out jets of thrust into space.

The fiery demise of Mentor and his machine is also very well handled.

Maya's shape shifting into various animal forms is generally very well done here, too. The use of real animals in certain scenes in the finale is very impressive.

The episode does not end with a light-hearted attempt at humour, either, but a more sombre and sober comment about the theme of season two.

By this I mean aliens and humans getting to know one another and learning to live together as friends. Maya is welcomed by John and Helena with the line "we're all aliens until we get to know each other", underscoring the idea that space opera is, fundamentally, a format which deals with the idea of racial and cultural diversity, both the conflicts and the alliances.

On the critical side, the episode perhaps fails to be about the plight of Moon base Alpha, the survival of the inhabitants, (a mainstay of season one) except as a backdrop to the drama on planet Psychon.

Perhaps the most disappointing thing is that Maya never gets to meet Tony, her future love interest, on screen. There is also no scene of her arriving on the Moon and being welcomed into Alpha base and introduced to the place that will become her new home.

Scenes such as these could have been saved for the beginning of the second episode, perhaps. But this does not happen, either. It seems a pity, particularly as the bond between Tony and Maya will become one of the main emotional under currents of the season.

Nevertheless, the episode ends dramatically, leaving us with a strong anticipation that we are about to see just what kind of new excitement Maya and her shape changing powers can bring to Moon base Alpha and its future adventures.

All in all this ranks as one of the strongest episodes of the second season and a very good way to launch the second year of *Space: 1999*.

One of the interesting things about the character of Maya is that although she is a shape shifter the character has an origin story which is extremely similar to that of DC comics' *Superman*.

Her planet, just like Superman's home planet Krypton, is doomed to be destroyed in a huge explosion and it is her father who is trying to save the planet and although her father does not put her in a rocket as a baby, she is ultimately entrusted to John and Helena and escapes the destruction of the planet by leaving in an Eagle spaceship just before the planet explodes.

Perhaps it would be more fitting to compare her to *Supergirl* and it is perhaps pertinent to note that in the TV promotional trailers released in the United States her character was promoted as the *Wonder Woman* of science fiction. The interesting thing about that is that this would have been a year or so before *Wonder Woman* actually appeared in a TV series on American television.

One sticking point for many fans of the series has been the concept of her ability to change shape and undergo metamorphosis into other life forms. I'm not sure exactly why some fans find it difficult to accept this concept since we had already seen characters undergo complete molecular transformation in season one. It happened twice to the alien who took over baby Jackie in 'Alpha Child' for example.

If Maya has the ability to convert all available matter into pure energy and reshape it at will then it is completely plausible that she could adopt different shapes and forms even down to the inclusion of the clothing which is being worn. We know that there is a great deal of space between molecules in matter.

If she is able to expand or contract the amount of space between molecules when she creates new structures, then she could obviously become very big or very small at will. The character is presented as something of a superhero. This comic book superhero feeling is slightly at odds with the science fiction feeling of the rest of the series.

However, some effort is made in episodes such as 'Space Warp' and the 'Dorcons' to add some complexity to Maya and suggest she could be dangerous to humans. Some back-story is also developed in her conversation with the Commander on planet Luton and her confrontation with her old friend Dorzac.

It is interesting to note that everyone on the base seems to view her as innocent of any involvement with her father and the atrocities committed in his attempts to save his planet. When she speaks highly of her father on planet Luton, the Commander listens but passes no apparent judgement. One thing almost universally agreed upon in fandom is that whatever people feel about the character, actress Catherine Schell played the part very well indeed and was perfectly cast in the role. Season two is very much the Maya era of *Space: 1999*.

MAYA'S COMPUTER

ANALYSIS

9/10

This is a solid episode which starts off the second season in style with a good introduction for alien Maya. Catherine Schell is immediately likeable and easy to warm to and the episode is an effective relaunch for the series. Byrne delivers a solid script and Johnson's effects are eye popping.

NEW TITLES SEQUENCE AND
NEW DIRECTION

It's a brand-new season and the first thing that hits you is the shiny new opening title sequence. The old one was so amazingly awesome, it's an automatic feeling of what a shame they changed something so good.

But the new titles are very good, all the same. They lack the excitement and icy menace of the originals, but with no "This Episode" montage of shots, there is no giving away what is to come. More unfortunate, perhaps, is the fact the new titles are up front, like they were with *UFO*, the precursor to *Space:1999*. This means we lose one of *Space:1999* year one's most enduring good points, the cold open.

Whatever the episode was like, in the first season, you could always be sure of one thing. The cold open, often beginning right in the middle of some action or drama, would grab you and get you hooked, in the most cutting-edge way, only to reach a cliffhanger and then go into the titles with the lead in of a menacing drum-roll.

This return to the style of *UFO*, where a standard title sequence comes in at the very start, does suggest that the new producer of *Space:1999* has a certain lack of showmanship.

The new producer is Fred Frieberger and his lack of panache flies in the face of his stated intentions to make a more exciting season than the first one, produced by outgoing producer Sylvia Anderson.

However, it seems plausible that Freddie was motivated by the wish to clarify some confusion about the show's premise and possibly wanted to do it from the very outset. The opening credits spell out the show's format, with typing text, much like the case of *UFO*. But unlike *UFO*, where the text was being typed on paper, with a golf ball typewriter, here the text is lettering on the imagery itself.

In big yellow letters, we are told that there is massive nuclear explosion near Moon base Alpha, that the Moon is torn out of Earth orbit and hurled into outer space.

The opening titles also introduce the new addition to the cast, Catherine Schell as Maya. We see images of Earthly wild animals in a close up of her eye. What that is all about at this point would be anyone's guess, but most advanced publicity for season two focused on the introduction of Maya to the series.

'The Metamorph' is a pretty good pilot episode for the second season. And although *Space:1999* began in season one, I think the term pilot episode is accurate here because season two is very much like a whole new show, albeit built upon the foundation of season one.

Many fans have, over the years, been vocal about the massive changes to *Space:1999* which are unveiled here.

But while you could be forgiven for thinking *Space:1999* has been not so much tweaked to polish and improve upon what went before, but tweaked with a sledgehammer, this is still very much the same show, despite the cosmetic make-over.

The more subtle changes are the ones which matter the most, yet they are the least obvious. Intellectualism and hard science fiction are sorely missed as cast members, titles sequence, incidental music and the Main Mission set.

This, then, is the pilot episode for a new kind of *Space:1999*, one which has different aims and intentions to season one. Yet, in fairness to the series, it is not as unrelated to season one as some of its detractors seem to believe.

In fact, this pilot is very much a continuation of season one, even as it prepares to introduce a whole new look and some new characters.

THE EXILES

When a swarm of space bees approaches Alpha, they turn out to be missile-like cylinders. Koenig and Maya bring one down and cut it open. It turns out these things are actually cryogenic containers with a frozen alien humanoid in each.

When the Alphans thaw a young man and young woman back to life, the pair use Alpha's power to project a space-time tunnel to their home planet, where they intend to exact a terrible revenge.

Taking Tony and Helena with them, the pair terrorize the descendants of those who exiled them for their sociopathic behaviour, until Koenig tricks the female alien and Helena finds a way to bring the male, Cantar, unstuck.

This is quite a good episode. However, it is probably not a very good choice for the second episode of the second season. As a follow-up to 'The Metamorph', it is a poor choice. A new season, particularly one which has changed the show so much, needs to really pull the viewers in. While this episode is not bad, it lacks the excitement factor needed to really grab the audience and bring them on-board.

It is certainly a good episode in its own right. It just does not deliver, however, on the promise of 'The Metamorph', the promise that alien Maya is going to bring new excitement to Alpha and the show.

It is not an episode which showcases Maya and her amazing shape changing powers. Maya is simply there. She is part of the crew, and her place seems to be already established, too.

She and Tony spend time together during the episode but there is no tantalising hints of a pair who have just met and are on the verge of realising that they have a strong attraction for each other. All the interesting stuff between Tony and Maya appears to have happened off-screen.

To follow up 'The Metamorph', one would expect one of Freddie's specially penned episodes which focus heavily on Maya and her powers to be screened as the second episode.

Or better still, Johnny Byrne's Maya-heavy episode 'The Dorcons' could have been screened as episode two. I've always argued against following strict production order. 'The Dorcons' would have been fascinating because it focuses on Maya but depicts her as something of a liability to the Alpha base, in some ways.

It shows her as someone that hostile aliens want to hunt down, aliens who are more than willing to pound the Moon base to rubble and ruin in order to get hold of her. To raise the question of whether or not adopting Psychon's last surviving daughter was a good idea or a bad one, might have added some welcome dramatic complexity.

On the other hand, an episode like the 'Beta Cloud' in which Maya saves Alpha or 'Space Warp', in which Maya is shown to be a dangerous liability to the base when she becomes ill, could have been interesting choices. I would still go with Dorcons because it shows an alien attack hammering the base and Eagles trying to fight back in a manner reminiscent of season one's 'War Games'. This could have been a strong way of showing fans that this is still the same show they knew and loved.

Alternatively, when the first season was shown in America, the episode 'Dragon's Domain' was screened as the second episode because it featured a monster. The same idea of kicking off with the monster story was used in the original *Star Trek* a few years earlier, with the episode The Man Trap kicking off the series.

The big monster story of season two is 'Bringers of Wonder'. As it's a two-part story with a cliffhanger ending to keep viewers coming back the following week, it would have made a great follow-up to 'The Metamorph'. By the end of 'Bringers of Wonder' viewers would be three episodes into the new season and quite possibly hooked enough to keep watching.

The theme of reconnecting with lost Earth would have been well established and then the episode 'Journey to Where' would have made a much greater impact as it features the Alpha crew finally discovering what really happened to Earth in the time since they broke away from Earth orbit and went on their odyssey through the galaxy.

Viewed simply as an episode in its own right, the Exiles is quite an interesting story, once it gets going. It has much in common with the season one story 'Earthbound'. As with 'Earthbound', it involves aliens awakened by the Alphans from cryogenic sleep.

But whereas the aliens in 'Earthbound' turned out to be friendly, the titular exiles are most definitely hostile. One of the interesting things about 'The Exiles' is that the script was originally written for the season one format and characters.

This seems to be apparent in the feel of the episode. It moves at a reasonably slow and deliberate pace and there is a lot of focus on procedure, both astronautic procedure and medical procedure.

The episode gives us some interesting insights into how the Alphans have harnessed the moon and its resources since leaving Earth orbit. They appear to have built a kind of laboratory into an underground cave, far beneath the moon's surface. It is here that the Alphans use an industrial laser to cut open an alien capsule which contains a cryogenically suspended alien.

This is one of many things in season two which hints that this new era of *Space:1999* is taking place a considerable amount of time after the end of season 1. (Some fans have noted that the day count given by Helena Russell in her log entries may clash with the facts, but I think these continuity issues can be overlooked and dismissed as human error.

I certainly doubt the production team expected anyone to take the day counts so seriously as to work out when each episode is mean to be taking place in an exact timeline, particularly as ITV shows had no fixed screening order.)

British actors Stacy Dorning and Peter Duncan play a pair of alien humanoids who appear to be in their late teens or early 20s. The theme of the story seems to focus on the idea of juvenile delinquents, people who have dropped out or rejected society, presumably adopted a free spirit attitude. However, they are also free of moral values and seem to think that killing is perfectly okay. Their characterisation reflects some of the things which were going on in the world in the late 1960s and early 1970s.

Followers of people such as Charles Manson, the members of his so-called Manson Family, had become a kind of anti-social cult and had committed horrific acts of violence and murder in the United States. This idea of callous and morally bankrupt adolescence comes through when the alien pair manipulate and scheme to get control of Alpha's power source so they can teleport themselves home, to their planet, Golos. Their aim is to confront those in authority on Golos and get revenge on them, punish the people who cast them out into the universe as exiles.

The model shots for Golos are typically good and the blue corridor through which they teleport is very well done for the period. The set for the interior of the Golos control area is decent and the humanoid aliens in their costumes are okay. It's a pity perhaps that the episode takes a long time to get to this alien planet. It might've been nice to get some other angles on the planet. The most obvious thing missing here is the typical situation where an Eagle visit the alien planet, but the teleportation plot makes this impossible. It certainly would've added another dimension to the portrayal of planet Golos to see an Eagle landing and humans heading out to explore. What we do get to see of Golos is quite good, all the same, if a little limited.

The finale of the episode contains a few welcome moments of horror, something which generally features much less in season two compared to season 1. This comes when Peter Duncan ages rapidly and horribly to death. A number of different make up effects sequences are used to suggest his rapid ageing and grotesque physical deterioration. Some of this is very good and there's even a weird, distorted shot, through a transparency, which adds to the nightmarish feel of the scene.

However, the episode is not without its flaws, as well. For some reason an American accented voice is dubbed onto Peter Duncan. It's not clear why this was done, but it was not an uncommon practice for actors to be looped at the time. It's often the case that audio quality is poor, but it has also happened when a producer has been unhappy with someone's accent or line delivery.

Possibly Duncan had attempted an American accent that the producers asked for but were not convinced by his efforts. Or perhaps his own British accent had struck the producer as something which would not appeal to American viewers.

For whatever reason, Duncan's voice is looped. In the finale, Dr Helena Russell taunts the rapidly ageing alien as she avoids his stolen laser. Barbara Bain's voice in this scene is a voice over, too, added onto the soundtrack in post-production. The effect is still reasonably convincing, in her case. But there is a feeling of cutting corners, with things like this. Koenig also had to contend with a voice from Brian Blessed's Mentor in the fiery climax of 'The Metamorph', too.

The British unions had a powerful stranglehold on film production techniques and methods in the 1970s, forcing all directors to work within strict schedules.

Everyone from *Doctor Who* directors and actors to Stanley Kubrick's crew from *Full Metal Jacket* are on record about the unionised manner in which British film crews were controlled, with endless lengthy tea breaks and ruthless cut off times. Producer Freddie Freiberger was, apparently, determined to get around their strict limitations on shooting schedules, by way of creative approaches to speeding up production.

202

There are times in the episode where Maya makes her presence felt, but these scenes feel like ideas from Fred Freiberger designed to showcase the character, rather than part of the natural story structure as written by the script writer.

As we know the script was written for the season one format, it seems logical to suppose Maya's added scenes were late additions. They feel somewhat bolted on and superfluous.

They are not exactly wonderful scenes, but we can see they intend to show the series now has room for a sense of humour in a way which was not apparent, at least to casual viewers and critics, during season one. They also showcase her abilities.

Unfortunately, there are times when we can clearly see on the screen that some episodes needed more time to shoot extra close-ups or cutaways or even do some re-shoots. When you are simply adding in the taunting or shouting as a voice over, it becomes apparent that production time was getting tight.

The old lady who commands on Golos is a bit of an underdeveloped character. She's also a bit easily panicked for a leader of a whole alien civilization, too, freaking out more like someone's old Granny than a nation's iron-willed leader when the sparks start to fly.

Despite these quibbles, 'The Exiles' is a reasonably good episode, particularly in the second half where Tony and Helena are transported to the aliens' home planet.

MAYA'S COMPUTER

ANALYSIS

8/10

Let down by some dubbed voices and some scenes which feel jammed in at the expense of the story, 'Exiles' is a strong episode, nevertheless. The themes of callous disenfranchised youth and some moments of horror make it worth watching. The guests are appealing, and it all feels very reminiscent of season one.

ONE MOMENT OF HUMANITY

Helena and Tony are abducted to a planet ruled by androids who have no imagination and need to trick the Earth people into demonstrating violence so they can learn how to kill their creators.

This script was written by Tony Barwick, the first of two contributions he makes to *Space:1999* this season.

In one of his last ever interviews, given in the late 1980s to a UK Sci Fi Magazine, Barwick explained that he was not asked to write for season one of *Space:1999* because the Americans wanted a more American set of writers.

While I think they certainly ended up with mostly British writers on year one, perhaps Barwick was indeed excluded for this reason. It's a pity, too, because he would've been a solid contributor. But it's also interesting to note that the absence of Barwick in season one gave the series a very different feel compared to *UFO* and the later puppet series.

Barwick had an impressive record, so this episode is one we can say is definitely written by one of Gerry Anderson's top writers. In fact, his first job for Gerry Anderson was on his puppet classic *Thunderbirds*. Most Anderson fans probably know this, but *Thunderbirds* began life as a half hour show. Lord Lew Grade, the backer, was so impressed, he asked for the episodes to be expanded to an hour. The first nine episodes were already made as half hours. Tony Barwick, under the guidance of Alan Fennell, had the task of expanding the half hour episodes by writing new material which could be added into them.

Barwick gave an interview in the late 1980s in which he explained the method was to add a sub plot, so something could happen on the way to the rescue. Barwick went on to become head writer and script editor on such Anderson classics as *Captain Scarlet* and *Joe 90* and finally *UFO*, where he contributed some greatly respected episodes such as 'Confetti Check-AOK', 'A Question of Priorities' and 'Mind Bender', which are often regarded as some of the best work to go out under the Anderson banner.

In his late 80s interview, Barwick explained his approach to television writing. His belief was that if you watch two minutes of a TV show, it should make you want to watch the next two minutes and so on. This approach seems evident in his scripts, which are notably tight in their crafting, focused in their plotting and rigorously logical. With this in mind, it's fair to say 'One Moment of Humanity' is a far cry from his best work, but with his hallmark style and well-honed skills as a script writer, it is never less than engaging and watchable.

Barwick did not make it clear if he was familiar with season one, but when pressed about *Space:1999*, he expressed a feeling the show was a little ordinary, that he would have tried to make it stranger, more bizarre, had he been the head writer. That being said, he delivers a solid if somewhat unremarkable story here, perhaps fulfilling his own sense of the series as a little pedestrian, at least as he perceived it.

The plot of the episode is a very oddball one, in a way, and contains many things I would not immediately expect from a Barwick script, so I can only assume this plot was some sort of contractual obligation and that many of the things in it were requested by the producers for reasons related to their new vision for the series. If this was the case, we might excuse Barwick for some of it as he may, in fact, have had no choice but to write this story.

One of the first things which strikes me as the intruding hand of producers is the opening scene of Maya and Helena playing dress-ups. The costume worn by Barbara Bain, an off the shoulder dress, which makes a striking contrast to her usual medical uniform, and the fact the plot focuses on her character ending up in a dance sequence, a sequence which becomes a seduction, really feel like deliberate attempts to glamorize Bain and her character.

Barbara Bain was a dancer before she became an actress and dance legend Lionel Blair was brought in to choreograph the seductive dance sequence for the episode's highly charged finale. Possibly the new producer Freddie wanted to have a script which could incorporate Bain's dancing skills and dance background into the plot.

As with his beginnings on *Thunderbirds*, Barwick may have been simply writing to order.

The plot itself seems to revolve around the idea that robots have no imagination and cannot do anything until they see a human do it first, so they can get the opportunity to copy and mimic it, including acts of violence.

The fact they resort to using jealousy and lust seems like another contractual obligation, presumably from Freddie, to focus on the emotional relationships between his lead characters. This episode should be unwatchable, given the oddball elements, but it's actually pretty involving and ends on quite a strong note.

Tony Barwick was Gerry Anderson's most experienced and prolific screen writer, who stayed with him from *Thunderbirds* through to *UFO* and came back for this season of *1999* and you can see here that he knows how to spin lead into gold. It's not his best script by any means, probably due to the shopping list of requirements he seems to have been asked to include or build a story around.

But at least he smuggles a few good things into the episode, notably a role for Geoffrey Bayldon. In the UK, Bayldon is something of a television legend, a brilliant character actor noted for the TV series *Catweazel*. He appeared on *Doctor Who* in 'Creature from the Pit' and would have been a great choice to play *Doctor Who*, a role he was apparently considered for at times.

As the humanoid who speaks to Helena and Tony, he does little more than speak exposition, but he is so good as a character actor that he manages to make his role seem both significant and sympathetic. If there's a regret about this episode, it is that Bayldon didn't get more screen time to develop a stronger sense of who he and his people are and why we should care if they are saved from the killer androids.

Another reason this odd episode works is because Charles Chrichton was a top director and he gives this story some solid structure and good, if not particularly great, pace. The strangest thing is, Freddie wanted to do away with what he saw as a static English show where people stand around waiting for things to happen. He wanted a focus on action.

While the episode certainly delivers on dance routines, Helena and Maya in feminine dresses and outfits, emotions about love and romance, etc, there is precious little action before the end. Martin Landau gets little enough to do before he finally gets to lose his pacifier and punch Zarl in the face at the end.

But it's another episode which does not end on a cheesy attempt at light-hearted comedy, so that's a definite plus. And Billie Whitelaw and Leigh Lawson are great guest stars, too.

MAYA'S COMPUTER

ANALYSIS

7/10

A story which has some good passages and good ideas but gets into rather silly territory at times. Held together by a good writer, good director, and some gifted guest stars. The fact Lionel Blair choreographed the dancing is a rare boast for a science fiction adventure series.

ALL THAT GLISTERS

Trapped on a dying planet with time running out before they need to get back to Alpha, John, Helena, Alan, Tony, Maya, and an oddball Alphan who thinks himself a cowboy of space must contend with an intelligent life form which is totally new to them – a living rock, capable of possessing Tony's body and using him for its own ends.

Faced with a story in which the Alphans come into contact with a totally alien life-form unlike anything on Earth (a living rock) and must struggle to understand the motives of this life form, which they cannot easily relate to or communicate with, the whole cast and crew of *Space:1999* decided it was awful and refused to do it.

It's not exactly clear what the objections were, but it seems Martin Landau disliked the way Koenig, and the other characters were portrayed, while the director apparently had an intense dislike of the living rock idea, even presenting a rock to the producer at the end of production as an ironic gift, after which he vowed to never work on the series again.

Despite the misgivings of these talented and well-intentioned people, in most important respects, 'All That Glisters' is actually a pretty great episode.

The set for the dying alien planet is suitably barren and dead-looking, yet still somehow looks beautiful. The fact it is the only episode with no scenes set on Alpha makes it very focused, like a kind of bottle episode. And the dramatic unity of this is so nice, I feel it's sad we were never treated to more stories set entirely on an alien planet like this.

Keith Miles was a prolific writer and novelist who wrote under different names and not some inexperienced hack who could not write. However, I assume a couple of lines were added by American producer Freddie to make it more Trek-like, which is unfortunate because a few lines stand out as clichéd or clunky.

But the plot about the Alphans struggling to find a way to communicate with a totally alien life force is very good, well focused, and ultimately suspenseful, as well.

The direction is intense, too, giving the episode a somewhat bizarre feel, almost like a weird, surreal nightmare, at times, particularly when the rock thing takes over the Eagle, trapping Helena and trying to fly off into space, leaving the others stranded.

Some of the FX have dated badly, such as the use of coloured spotlights, but the Eagle blast off from the planet still looks superb. Despite the fact the director and Fred didn't see eye to eye, his last directing job on the series is really very good, with solid pacing and menacing atmosphere.

I'm not sure why the cast and crew were so down on it. I suspect Landau may have taken Koenig's indecision as a sign of being a poor leader, rather than a conflicted one who is faced with a life form, and a situation, which he is not sure about.

'All That Glisters' is one of *Space: 1999*'s most notorious episodes because the fact the script raised the ire of actor Martin Landau was eventually made public.

According to actor Tony Anholt in an interview given in the 1980s, Producer Freddie Freiberger decided to dig his heels in and insist the episode be made, even though Martin Landau and the cast initially refused to do it.

Landau describes the characters as shmucks and says his own character takes a beating in the episode. Anholt described Fred Freiberger as a very stubborn man who refused to budge, apparently arguing this was the most sci fi episode of them all and must be made.

He also said Landau capitulated because he didn't want to affect the cast and crew for whom the episode was a paid job of professional work.

It seems strange watching the completed episode to think that the drama behind-the-scenes was so intense. It's actually a pretty good episode, if viewed with an open mind. It's not perfect but it definitely has its merits.

Some of the dialogue definitely feels like it was added to make the series more like *Star Trek* in flavour. This was possibly done by Freddie acting as a script editor.

A more sympathetic, less combative, situation behind the scenes could have led to some tweaking. Alas, when a cast and director dislike a script, it seems to take away from the end result. Landau does seem to take the opportunity to vent some anger in a few scenes, however, which seems to add to the feeling of dramatic intensity, if nothing else!

However, while it's true that some character motivations and dialogue could arguably be better, it should be noted that many writers say that dialogue is simply the icing on the cake while storytelling, in essence, is not dialogue. It is structure. It is the actual plot.

Breaking Bad's Vince Gilligan and others have gone on the record saying that structure is everything in storytelling. In terms of story structure, this one is focused and intense.

What's more the episode achieves a sense of bizarre, twisted, nightmare which is highly enjoyable to watch. Despite the director's misgivings, silicone life forms are common tropes in science fiction. The most obvious analogy to this plot would be the *Star Trek* episode 'Devil in the Dark'. However, the episode does not really bare close resemblance to its *Star Trek* counterpart. Nor does it feature an actor on all fours, covered in a rubber mat, crawling around the set.

Silicone based life forms have appeared on *Doctor Who* in episodes such as 'Hand of Fear' and 'The Stones of Blood'. They also featured in such *Outer Limits* episodes as 'Moon Stone' and 'Corpus Earthling'. It seems strange therefore that *Space: 1999*'s living rock episode should be greeted with such outright hostility.

In *Space: 1999* terms, the plot is quite similar to season one's 'Space Brain' episode where another Alphan was taken over by a glowing, multi-coloured mass of alien life and the Alphans struggled to communicate or understand its true motives.

And while 'All That Glisters' has its faults; it is notable that 'Space Brain' was the episode in which Moon Base Alpha was flooded by piles of foam. Both episodes require a certain willingness from the audience to suspend disbelief if they are to be appreciated and enjoyed.

A final note should be made about the guest appearance of actor Patrick Mower. Mower was known for portraying tough secret agent types in series such as *Callan* and Special Branch and had played the rather creepy Cass Fowler on the *UFO* episode "The Square Triangle. Here, however, he has a rare chance to be a funny and offbeat, good guy for a change.

The fact his space cowboy persona is obsessed with Texas and all things Wild West yet has an Irish accent and is defined as an Irish Cowboy suggests there may have been some creative compromise in the way the character developed. Possibly Mower's Dave was meant to be a Texan, but Mower felt unable to do a convincing Texan accent.

While oddball, Dave is actually a pretty interesting character. At the outset he seems fascinated by Maya, something which makes Tony rather territorial. He also seems to have a one-track mind when he gets intrigued by the notion of the living rock.

However, his character rises above this as the episode progresses. He seems to feel hurt that Maya, along with the rest, think the rock is all he cares about. Foolhardy or not, he sets out to prove that he really does care for his fellow Alphans and frees Tony and Helena in the end, from the Eagle where they are trapped.

He also attempts to fight the living rock with his laser. He fails and is taken over, but Koenig ultimately succeeds in blasting the rock and dehydrating it. In the end, I can't help but like Dave.

And the living rock, which only wanted to survive, is ultimately given its chance thanks to the departing Alphans.

Red may be dead, and they might all be schmucks, but this is actually a bizarre, trippy, and terse little excursion into the realms of 70s sci-fi and a trip worth taking.

And Brian Johnson choosing to use gold tinsel streaming from the underside of an Eagle to depict the cloud seeding, when Maya plays rain maker, is a lovely visual touch at the end.

MAYA'S COMPUTER

ANALYSIS

7/10

Despite its flaws, Ray Austin and the talents of Patrick Mower bring real intensity to this bizarre, oddball slice of waking nightmare. Genuinely compelling, almost in spite of itself. Some of the visuals are truly striking. Some of the dialog, however, is rather dire. Not the disaster of legend but an enjoyable oddity.

JOURNEY TO WHERE

Earth makes contact. The Alphans can return home, by matter transference. But when Koenig, Helena and Alan try it, things go awry and they end up on Earth, but displaced back in time.

They are in Scotland and as Helena succumbs to viral pneumonia, they are captured by locals who wonder if they have been infected with the plague and turned out to die.

This is an excellent episode. 'Journey to Where' stands apart from the rest of the season in a way that only a handful of other episodes do. The plot is very different from everything else around it.

But 'Journey to Where' probably appears in the wrong place in the season order however because it is the episode in which the people of Alpha finally make contact with planet Earth again. It is the episode where the inhabitants of the Moon base find out what happened to the Earth.

Since 'Bringers of Wonder' involves a visit by what appears to be visitors from Earth as the Alphans remember it, only to have it turn out to be an illusion, 'Journey to Where' probably should come after 'Bringers of Wonder'. That way the audience who are left wondering what really happened to Earth after the 'Breakaway' at the end of 'Bringers' can finally find out.

In fact, if 'Bringers of Wonder' had screened soon after 'The Metamorph', 'Journey to Where' would have been a very welcome follow-up for answering the questions viewers were left with about what really happened to Earth and its people, what is the situation really like on Earth now, etc.

The episode opens with a voice echoing through space calling Moon Base Alpha. The voice indicates that the transmission uses neutrinos to cross cosmic distances. Koenig is suspicious and checks the authenticity of the message first by asking for background information on the science of neutrinos and then by asking questions about such things as the first man in space and the American World Series.

This means the episode begins with a sense of hard science fiction, with facts and names overtly mentioned, as well as some charm.

In this regard the episode immediately puts the viewer back in the mindset or feel of season one, where the hard science fiction vibe was a big part of the show's appeal.

'Journey to Where' introduces an idea which has not really been attempted on *Space: 1999* before this point, at least by the humans. For the first time the Alphans will travel across space not by Eagle ship but by teleportation and matter transmitter, using a device they themselves create.

Of course, various aliens have used matter transmission in previous episodes such as 'The Exiles' and first season episodes such as 'Guardian of Piri' and 'Ring Around the Moon', but with advice from Earth, the Alphans construct a transference dome and a matter transmission cubicle.

One of the things which makes the episode a real winner is that John, Helena and Alan Carter are the three people who go on the journey. This focus on the three main characters who have been in the series from the very beginning gives the episode a feeling of authenticity.

One of the interesting things about the episode is the depiction of Earth.

Earth, it is revealed to us in the story, has been rendered almost completely lifeless and uninhabitable, in the time since the 'Breakaway' of the Moon, the surface of the planet laid waste by the pollution of the 21st century. This rather dire prediction of what could happen to Earth as a result of runaway pollution and waste is very interesting because it ties into popular fears which were common in science fiction in the mid-70s and seems ahead of its time when viewed today.

It further adds to and supports the depiction of the Moon and the Moon base as a kind of Noah's Ark for Mankind, travelling to the stars in search of a new home and leaving behind planet Earth made almost like the moon itself by Man's own careless use of industrialisation and technology.

The cities in which the human survive now are giant domes atop cylindrical towers, shaped like transparent mushrooms. The model work for these cities of the future is very impressive and well done. Surprisingly, the depiction of the technology used by the humans of the future is very imaginative for the era in which the series was produced. For example, the humans are shown to be using clear or transparent flat screens.

This seems to have been achieved in a very simple manner. Data and numbers and other computer icons are put on to the flatscreen simply by reflecting from a video monitor, which is out of shot. It's the same technique used for teleprompters read by newsreaders. But the visualisation is excellent. Even today, transparent flat screens for laptops and PCs are still relatively new and cutting-edge technology.

When the Alphan party are teleported and they find themselves back on Earth, the scenes are filmed on location at Black Park, which adds further to the high-quality feeling of this episode. Instead of aliens, robots or monsters the menace here turns out to be hostile humans in 13th century Scotland. This is the type of thing *Space:1999* does very well.

One of the main guest stars is Roger Bisley. He is an excellent actor with a great on-screen presence. He is well known to fans of British cult science fiction for an appearance in the science fiction series *The Tomorrow People*. In *The Tomorrow People* he played the second incarnation of Jedikiah, a shape changing robot villain. Here, he plays a Scotsman who takes John, Helena and Alan prisoner.

Freddie Jones and Isla Blair also appear. Many British viewers apparently disliked Jones doing an American accent in the episode, but as an Australian who had not seen him in other work, I actually thought he was a genuine American. Isla Blair had played an alien in season one's 'War Games' episode, so it is good to see her back in another role. In 'War Games' she sounded British, here she too adopts an American accent. In 'War Games' she was bald, here she wears a platinum blonde wig.

The episode introduces a subplot where Helena becomes ill. This affords Barbara Bain the opportunity to deliver her finest dramatic performance of *Space: 1999*'s second season. Her concern for John's safety and her heartbreak as she realises the situation she finds herself in, with viral pneumonia, is brilliantly and courageously acted.

Martin Landau also excels in his scenes with Helena and his concern for her is palpable. We really get the clear impression that John and Helena have fallen in love, and they are deeply fearful of losing each other.

The character of Alan Carter has the opportunity to charm us once more with his Aussie personality. This includes singing 'fly me from the moon at last' and 'fire, fire, burn so bold'. Although actor Nick Tate apparently did not like the fact that Fred Freiberger wanted him singing in the series, it provides some charm and comic relief. It is also a fitting call back to the season one episode 'Death's other Dominion', in which Alan sings 'Pack up your troubles' while lost in the snow on the planet Retha.

The dialogue is excellent in the scene where John and Alan realise that they are back on Earth. Helena cries hysterically that she can see the moon in the sky. Koenig initially dismisses it as one of many possible moons the planet could have. But he and Alan soon recognise features on the lunar surface and name them.

This evokes the hard science fiction feel which people generally associate with *Space: 1999*, once again. Alan and John also mention the 'Breakaway' and finally conclude they are on Earth sometime in the past. These overt references to the 'Breakaway' and the lunar landmarks help sell the story convincingly and intelligently.

The use of Morse code in the finale is another nice touch. Also good is the fact that the Alphans are almost burnt at the stake for being plague *Carrier*s by their Scottish captors. When they are teleported to safety at the last moment the audience is left to wonder if the shocked and disbelieving inhabitants of 13th century Scotland will interpret this as the work of Satan or perhaps some form of magic or witchcraft.

The episode ends on a particularly thoughtful and well-written note in which the Commander recites a litany of terrible incidents from human history they could have found themselves involved in. The final line of the episode has Helena saying, 'with a history like that, who wants to go back to Earth anyway?'

Once again this would've been an excellent final comment had 'Journey to Where' been screened a week or so after 'Bringers of Wonder' in which the Alphans wrestle with their own longing to return to Earth.

We might've benefitted from 'The Taybor' being lodged in between 'Bringers' and 'Journey', since it also is an episode which deals with the home sick Alphans and their muted but earnest wish to return home to mother Earth. It would be nice to see the theme of longing for home played out as something of a thematic arc, with Helena's realisation that Earth is, perhaps, not all it's cracked up to be after all, as a final closing comment.

However, judged on its own merits there is no denying that 'Journey to Where' is an exceptionally strong and enjoyable episode and one of the true highlights of *Space: 1999*'s underrated second season.

A final thought: Imagine if this had been screened as episode 48 instead of 'The Dorcons'. It's the very last episode and we find out Earth, since the 'Breakaway', has become about the same as Alpha, a dead rock where people survive inside sealed enclosures. What a final twist or final revelation that would have made!

MAYA'S COMPUTER

ANALYSIS

10/10

One of the best episodes of the second season, this is a journey well worth taking. Future Earth is well realised and fascinating, the plot intriguing and the historical aspect very well done. A definite highlight of the season.

LOVING THE ALIEN

Catherine Schell in her distinctive make up, with notably curled and bumpy eyebrows and iconic sideburn like brown patterns on the skin, her auburn hair variously styled to enhance her classically beautiful face, is the most important and memorable addition to *Space:1999* in its second season.

The New York office of ITC had a great interest in Catherine Schell. She had already appeared on Space in the season one classic 'Guardian of Piri', making a lasting impression on fans as the sexy and seductive siren who was known as the servant of the Guardian.

But ITC New York was keen to see her in *Space:1999* as a major regular character. These ITC people were mainly a group of salesmen, and it may be presumed they saw Ms Schell as a strong selling point. Many fans of season one have been vocal about their dislike of the addition of the Maya character to the series.

But the truth is, without Maya there would have been no second season of *Space:1999*. The first season had sold well and rated well in the American market, but part of the funding had come from Italy's RAI.

RAI had presumably invested because *UFO*, the series which Space evolved from, had been a huge success in Italy. However, Space had proven less popular in Italy.

Season two would be funded purely by ITC on a smaller budget than season one. And the green light was only given when Gerry Anderson and Fred Freiberger came up with Catherine Schell's character of Maya.

Even if the series was not *Space: 1999*, Maya was an exciting enough idea to market and sell: a Wonder Woman from outer space with the power to change shape into animals, monsters and even other people, a character who could save the day and fight all comers.

It was the popular appeal of this character and the casting of Ms Schell which sealed the deal for *Space:1999* season two. Such a breakout character was Maya, there was even serious discussion of giving her a spin off series of her own after season two was in the can.

THE ROLE OF WOMEN IN SCIENCE FICTION

People often champion *Star Trek* for its politics, notably for depicting people of different races and both genders working together as equals. So, it's noteworthy that Maya is an alien crew member, not unlike Spock, but Maya is a woman. She is an intelligent, strong, brave, and powerful woman who saves Alpha on many occasions.

It is also noteworthy that Barbara Bain's Helena Russell, not Landau's Koenig, is the one who does season two's Alpha status reports, an equivalent of Kirk's Captain's log from *Trek*. This was only around five years on from Trek and two significant elements of *Trek* were being done by women instead of male characters, in *Space: 1999*.

It's never really been mentioned as far as I'm aware but season two of *1999* represents a significant shift in focus to strong female roles in TV science fiction. In the case of Helena's status reports, they seem to have evolved naturally from her case file narration of one of season one's most popular stories, 'Dragon's Domain'. For furthering the portrayal of women in science fiction, Maya and Helena deserve some recognition for their important contribution to the second season of this series.

THE TAYBOR

Mysterious objects appear on the Moon Base, presaging the arrival of Taybor, a larger-than-life character who travels through hyperspace in his ship, trading his wares and collecting things of beauty.

Little do the Alphans know, his latest fixation is with the beauty of their resident alien, Maya.

'The Taybor' is a very simple and light-hearted episode on the face of it. Although heavily made up, the guest actor Willoughby Goddard is actually a character actor of considerable note, even though you may not recognise him here.

His performance in this episode is funny, if grotesque. And his comeuppance at the end is made all the better by a guest appearance from Rita Webb, a very talented comedy actress who had appeared on comedy series such as the Benny Hill show (where she often played ill-tempered Mother-in-Law types).

But the episode has far more going for it than its face value might suggest.

Firstly, it is clearly a script written by someone with a strong, literate sense of the science fiction genre and its tropes and terminology. There are many interesting moments in the script to take note of. Firstly, this script joins 'Bringers of Wonder' and

'Journey to Where' in dealing with the same homesickness theme and the Alphans' longing for lost Earth which was suggested in season one episodes like 'Earthbound' and 'Another Time, Another Place'.

The Alphans offer Taybor everything in order to get a chance to return home to Earth. Taybor kidnaps the Commander and whisks him into hyperspace for a section of the episode running time, too.

It's a pity that the episode is only a single hour, in light of this sub-plot. While this may not seem a strong enough storyline to be made into a two-part story, on the face of it, there is a lot of potential which goes unexplored, here. Taybor suggests going to another planet for a few drinks or taking Koenig to the zoo, and even jokingly threatens to take him to be sold off at the slave markets on a planet called Shamanol.

There actually was a scene in an episode of *Blake's 7* a few years later in which the character of Kerr Avon (Paul Darrow) is auctioned at a slave market. Having seen the potential for humour in that scene on *Blake's 7*, it might have been a lot of fun to see Taybor actually try to sell Koenig at a slave market on an alien planet with various aliens bidding on him for various reasons.

It might also have been a lot of fun if we had seen Taybor take Koenig to a *Star Wars* style cantina full of aliens for a few drinks. And just imagine how much fun this episode could have become if Taybor had actually managed to take John Koenig back to modern-day Earth. We could have had some amazing scenes of Koenig back on Earth, accompanied by the bizarre looking alien Taybor. We might imagine the humour in Koenig attempting to explain away the strange and grotesque appearance of his alien friend once he finds himself back on Earth.

If these scenes had been filmed in England, it might have been funny to see Koenig, dressed in his Moon Base Alpha uniform, in an English village, perhaps, trying to get a telephone call through to the International Lunar Finance Commission, only to find they don't believe he is the real Koenig because he and Alpha are listed as missing in deep space, presumed dead.

The script, as it stands, is filled with interesting attempts at humour, a few of which are fairly funny.

When Taybor refers to a space restaurant as having a two-starburst rating from the Gourmet's Guide to the Galaxy, I found myself wondering if the late Douglas Adams was a fan of this episode.

This impression was further provoked by the marvellous dialog when Taybor gives Helena some perfume, describing it as the essence of a planet called Hermosia. This essence had been harvested by a fleet of robot spaceships while its sun was going super nova. He tells her it is called Infidelity, a name which is fitting when you consider what became of the planet's life-giving orb.

This is such a great piece of absurdist science fiction; it could almost be an entry in the electronic Hitch Hiker's guidebook itself.

When the episode gets into its second half it focuses on the idea that Taybor is essentially an ugly man, and this is why he surrounds himself with things of beauty. When Maya gives him his just deserts, the episode makes its point clear. Beauty may be only skin deep, but ugliness goes right through you.

The writer also introduces the notion of hyperspace travel to *Space:1999* in this episode. There is an interesting exchange between Taybor and Koenig in which Taybor says that Alpha is the first intergalactic moon he has ever come across. Koenig seems to be addressing the central mystery of how the moon has managed to travel so far from Earth. His comment is that he cannot explain it, but there have been space warps and other phenomena.

Taybor compares this to his own spaceship's ability to hyper jump. "So, you too jump", he says and mentions the little doorways in the sky. This is more overt than season one's implications, because it makes it plain that the moon drifts at sub light speeds yet crosses vast interstellar distances by undergoing occasional, random jumps, which cover many light years when it encounters natural openings in the fabric of space and time, doorways through hyperspace.

At one point in the episode there is a scene which is perhaps one of the lesser moments in the episode in which Taybor becomes drunk and passes out from drinking Tony Verdeschi's beer.

Although this scene is not one I particularly like, it does contain one of the few genuine moments of humour about Maya and her shape changing abilities. Taybor puts a hand on her thigh and says that this is a sign of friendship on his planet. Maya responds by putting her own hand on Taybor's thigh, but her hand transforms into a scaly green reptilian claw and Taybor gasps in wide-eyed pain, as the claws dig into is skin. Maya smiles and says, "now we are friends".

All in all, 'The Taybor' is an inconsequential, but fun episode. It is unlikely to be at the top of anyone's list of best or favourite *Space: 1999* episodes. But for its literate comments on how the moon travels the universe, its 'Hitch Hiker's Guide to the Galaxy' style of world building comments and for tapping once again into the sense of the Alphans as lonely and home sick wanderers who are still pining for the lost connection they once had with planet Earth, it is an episode of some value.

When we consider that this season spends four episodes, the two-part 'Bringers of Wonder', this episode and 'Journey to Where' dramatising the Alphans's longing to reconnect with Earth, it can be said that their homesickness is a major theme in season two. If 'Bringers' shows us the people the Alphans lost and 'Journey' shows us what Earth has become since the 'Breakaway', Taybor's wish to trade his jump drive for Maya poses the question of what price the Alphans would be prepared to pay for the chance to go home.

One interesting point about this is that Taybor quotes the Rhyme of the Ancient Mariner. *Alone, alone, all alone, alone on a wide, wide sea.* He describes the universe is a big place in which to wander, a big place in which to be lost. This helps to emphasise the notion that the Alphans are lost and alone in the vastness of the cosmos.

It's a nice counterpoint to their longing for Mother Earth which they have left behind.

MAYA'S COMPUTER
ANALYSIS
7/10

It may not be a very interesting or original plot and Taybor may look very silly, but this is a fun, generally enjoyable script by a writer who understands SF. There is much in the way of clever dialog and Goddard turns in a solid and likeable performance as the offbeat and amusing alien troublemaker.

THE RULES OF LUTON

Alone on a forest planet, John and Maya are accused by a voice from the trees of killing intelligent, sentient plant-life. They are confronted by three aliens who are to be their adversaries in a duel to the death. The survivors will win their freedom.

Writing under the name Charles Woodgrove, Fred Freiberger delivers the first of three self-scripted adventures for *Space:1999*, presumably to nail down his own vision of the series as an action-adventure series in outer space.

It's essentially an extended chase episode, modelled very loosely on Frederick Brown's classic science fiction short story Arena, which had previously been adapted unofficially as 'Fun and Games' on *The Outer Limits*, officially adapted as 'Arena' for *Star Trek* and would again be unofficially and loosely adapted as 'Duel' on *Blake's 7*.

The episode kicks off rather well with Koenig and Maya, easily the two most compelling leads in season two, stranded together on a planet which is decidedly verdant and Earth-like, as Tony heads back to Alpha due to an Eagle malfunction. The pair pick a flower and eat a berry and before you can say *Day of the Triffids*, it turns out this is a planet of intelligent plant life.

A booming voice rings out from all around, accusing them of terrible crimes and promising a terrible and well-deserved punishment.

This fast set up to kick things off is typical of Freiberger's grasp of pace, one of the genuine strengths of his storytelling.

Actor Roy Marsden is world famous these days for his portrayal of Inspector Adam Dalgliesh and well regarded for his role in *The Sandbaggers* too. It is surprising to realise one of his early acting roles was the non-speaking part as the invisible alien with a face like the Egyptian God Isis in this episode.

The speaking part in the episode goes to David Jackson, just a couple of years before he became famous as the gentle giant Gan in the BBC space adventure series *Blake's 7*. Jackson does have a very good speaking voice and he also provides the voice of the judges of Luton.

This episode is not only compared by many fans to the *Star Trek* episode 'Arena' because of its trial by combat plot but it is also compared by many to the *Lost in Space* episode 'The Great Vegetable Rebellion'.

While it is true that the initial moment where Koenig and Maya unwittingly upset intelligent plant life is similar to an early moment in the *Lost in Space* episode, I feel this comparison is highly unfair, on the whole.

In the *1999* episode, the judges are merely a disembodied voice and the only sign that the plants and trees on the planet are different to those on Earth is a few moments where they seem to sway and move in the finale and a moment where creeper vines try to ensnare Maya as a bird.

By comparison the *Lost in Space* episode features a man dressed as a gigantic carrot. It also features Dr Smith transforming into a gigantic stick of celery. A disembodied voice, over images of trees, seems mild and restrained by comparison to the ludicrous excesses of 'The Great Vegetable Rebellion'.

What makes the episode worth watching is the characterisation of the Commander and Maya, the excellent direction of director Val Guest and Martin Landau's strong, committed acting performance.

In the hands of a lesser actor, this could have been a very light weight and silly episode, but Landau seems determined to bring out the idea that the combat with the alien pursuers is gradually taking a tough physical and mental toll on his character.

Director Val Guest was famous for his work with Hammer films and seems to be on the same page as Landau.

It was not common to use a lot of blood and gore on television in the 1970s, so this is not exactly John Rambo in *First Blood*, but we do see Martin Landau injured and bleeding and becoming delirious and falling painfully down the hillside towards his final confrontation with the main alien adversary.

The episode is infamous for the fact that the American producer named the planet after a road sign he saw while driving in the UK. The planet's name is the same spelling therefore as a small place in England, but it is pronounced very differently.

The stress or emphasis in pronunciation is given to the second syllable in the episode whereas viewers living in England know the same name but with all of the word stress or emphasis on the pronunciation of the first syllable.

Since the Alphans were terrorised by a space probe from a plant called Triton in the first season and Triton is also the name of one of the moons of planet Neptune in real life, it seems only fair to say that perhaps that name similarity between the planet and the place in England is simply a coincidence.

But the behind-the-scenes story is quite funny, nevertheless.

One of the fascinating aspects of the story is that there is a very lengthy discussion between the two characters of Maya and the Commander. In these lengthy exchanges the pair reveal much about their own backstory.

In the case of the Commander, we learn that he was presumably an orphan since he had no one in his life other than a wife. We also learn that his wife was killed in a global conflict in the late 1980s.

The conflict was not a war in the traditional sense but a clash of race, religion, and differences. This appears to be introduced to create a parallel with the situation on the planet where plants and animals have been at war and now our heroes are in a conflict with other aliens.

The finale of the episode is very well done with the Commander using a bolo to take down his alien adversary. Perhaps intentionally tying into the theme that people killing people just because they are different is disgusting and wrong, Koenig looks to Maya when the voice of the judge shouts to kill.

She shakes her head, and he refuses and declares, 'I will not kill'. The indignant anger and rage of the Commander as he berates the judges at the end is really very good and again Martin Landau takes the opportunity to give some very strong acting. Even his 'never pick a flower' comment at the end of the episode seems rather nice.

MAYA'S COMPUTER

ANALYSIS

7/10

Another episode which seems to entertain almost in spite of itself. It may be easy to laugh at Luton and its talking plants, but there's some good stuff to enjoy here. Landau and Schell are on very good form, the direction is solid, and the themes are worthwhile and developed with considerable detail in the backstories.

THE MARK OF ARCHANON

Deep below Alpha, Alan Carter finds a hidden burial chamber from long ago in the moon's past. A man and boy are in suspended animation.

When they awaken, their secret problem, the so-called killing sickness, turns the alien man to violence.

Meanwhile Alan befriends the alien boy. As the alien man's behaviour gradually changes, he becomes a threat to the Alphans, ultimately taking Dr Russell hostage.

'The Mark of Archanon' is another of the rather weird cases of an episode where you really have to wonder if Fred Freiberger was aware of what was going on.

Considering his agenda was to feature fast-paced adventure stories with lots of action and heroics, focusing on monsters and Maya, with a dose of comic relief and some romance stuff to humanise the format characters, it seems very odd to get a plot like this one.

Here we have a very overtly symbolic tale of pacifist aliens who have visited Earth in the past and found it a place of violence, war and shocking brutality. And when I say symbolic, one of the aliens is afflicted by something called The Killing Sickness which turns them homicidal faster than you can say *obvious metaphor*.

The alien man is even named Pasc. Yes, Pasc the pacifist. From the planet of the Peace Bringers. There's a theme here, in case you may have missed it.

Now, it is understandable if viewers watching this episode feel the whole theme of peace and pacifism versus the sickness which is the impulse to kill is a little heavy handed, a little preachy and overblown, but it is nevertheless a far cry from hairy monsters played by stunt men and endless brawls with the Alpha security forces.

At least it has something to say, something for us to think about. It's an episode which feels like it comes from the mind of a writer who is genuinely thoughtful and wants to use the show's format to deal with themes of importance.

John Standing is very good in the role of the alien man and although his son Etrec is another actor to suffer the overdubbing of his voice by a professional voice artist, his bonding with Alan Carter is charming and endearing and another case of Nick Tate getting more to do than press buttons and say 'copy', which is very welcome indeed.

The aliens come dressed in a style that evokes ancient cultures such as the Egyptians and their hieroglyphics, but a female of the same race arrives in a huge spaceship and looks rather like the Queen of the Nile herself, Cleopatra. This is an interesting touch and as with year one's 'Ring Around the Moon', taps into the ancient astronaut's idea which was big in 1970s pop culture thanks to Yuri Geller and his fascinating, if poorly reasoned, *Chariots of the Gods*. If we are meant to assume the aliens visited Earth in the time of the Egyptians is not clear, but they had come to Earth and they had been suspended in cryo stasis under the moon for a very long time, so it is possible.

The episode features some horrific implications mixed with more symbolism or metaphor as Etrec seems to cut his own forehead to extract blood for the Alphans to examine and there are some white birds in one scene which could represent the dove of peace.

Koenig, meanwhile, is away in space, enduring an asteroid storm. While it's an excuse to get rid of the Commander and Maya so they can be free to shoot another episode, this is still fairly cool as we see their Eagle struggling through spinning asteroids. And while the asteroids themselves are just balls of scrunched up tin foil with some red lighting, it is very much a highlight of the episode when a big one comes at the Eagle and the Commander blasts it to bits with a laser beam.

Not the most exciting episode and a little lacking in subtlety, 'Mark of Archanon' is nonetheless an interesting episode which continues to show some intelligence, develop the idea of the Alphans tunnelling under the Moon and a nice chance to see more of Nick Tate's Alan Carter than usual.

MAYA'S COMPUTER

ANALYSIS

6/10

There are good intentions here and some intelligent and charming aspects, but this Eagle never takes off. However, the patient viewer will find some merit, thanks to a good theme and a pair of decent guest performers.

BRIAN THE BRAIN

The Moon is pulled off its trajectory by an unknown force and a spaceship appears. As Eagles intercept, a voice comes through, child-like, comical and claiming to be from a lost Earth expedition. Who is Brian and what really happened to his crew? When John and Helena are abducted into space, they find the answers.

This episode has some fun to it, but it feels a little stretched in the middle. I do like Brian but some of his psychotic dialog is a little too nasty. Having said that, it has the legendary Bernard Cribbins in it, so it's a must watch.

Cribbins is well known for many great roles and distinguished himself in the role of Donna's Grandfather Wilfred in the David Tennant era of *Doctor Who*. As a young man, he appeared in the Peter Cushing movie *Doctor Who: Daleks Invasion Earth:2160 A.D.*

Here he is the creator of 'Brian the Brain' and also provides the voice, which sounds like an impersonation of American comedian Jerry Lewis.

The episode begins quite well with something mysterious drawing the moon off its trajectory in space and there are quite a lot of nice shots of Alpha being evacuated. It's a very season one type of beginning to the story with alarms ringing through the base, people running and getting into action and lots of Eagles blasting off and heading up into space because the moon is on 'Collision Course' with something dangerous.

The episode continues to impress as it shows lots of nice visual effects work from Brian Johnson of Eagles heading out into space and the approach of a Swift from Earth. The interesting thing about Swift is that the craft is presumably the basic form of the more advanced Super Swift which appears in the episode 'Bringers of Wonder', but which according to the humans never got off the drawing board.

As is often the case with television science fiction of the 60s and 70s, episodes which begin mysteriously tend to lose a lot of their intrigue once the mystery is revealed.

The voice which cuts in from the Swift is unexpectedly comical and the dialogue lighthearted and jokey. We get a nice landing shot of the Swift. But when the crew of the base go aboard, they seem to find a deserted pilot section. The interior of the swift seems to be the same set which was used for the interior of Voyager 1 re-dressed slightly.

One of the interesting things about the robot or mobile computer called Brian is that he seems to be designed to look like part of the control consoles or computer banks in the ship. He then unexpectedly rolls forward and reveals that he is not a computer bank but a mobile machine with a mind of his own.

One of the problems with the episode is that Brian just isn't as funny or charming as he is supposed to be and nor is he a particularly interesting or exciting sci-fi robot creation either. He is just a little lame and forgettable.

His dialogue when he reveals his true colours is a little excessive too. Rather than seeming villainous or threatening, he comes across as a nasty vindictive little sadist.

The test seen with John and Helena in air locks is involving but ultimately a little bit on the nose. It seems a bit overstated. However, the end of the episode where Helena says, "it is a test we failed" and John says "I thought we passed it" with a hint of indignation and a smile, is one of the few times in the season when the humorous ending really works well.

This is because it feels right for their characters and Martin Landau really plays it perfectly.

Overall, this is an interesting episode. There is no Alan Carter in it, but you can't have everything. The spaceship design of the Swift is very similar to the Eagles (deliberately so, which would make sense) but we are not told of Brian's eventual fate: presumably he was set free in space with the Swift to explore the universe, this time with a set of Alphan morals. All in all, it's a fun episode if you are in the right mood for it.

MAYA'S COMPUTER

ANALYSIS

7/10

A bit silly? Yes, it is, to an extent. But fun to watch? Generally, yes, if you are open to it. Plus, Bernard Cribbins brings his legendary presence to the screen and there are some good model effects once again, with Eagles in large numbers. A pretty decent episode all round.

NEW ADAM NEW EVE

God turns up on Moon Base Alpha, or at least a man who claims to be God, in this first script for *Space:1999* by Terrence Feely. Feely is one of my favorite writers, due in large part to his classic episode of *UFO* called 'Timelash', which is often regarded as the best episode of that series for its pace, suspense and clever plot structure. Feely is a master of suspense and a man who writes terrific dialog. In 'Timelash', the main baddie, Turner, had the power to control time, at will, moving back and forth in time and toying with the Commander of SHADO.

Here, Feely presents us with another super powered villain. This time, he goes into more detail about how the troublemaker gets his power. He has an implant, some form of crystal, on his brainstem. The device is explained by Maya as a "light decelerator", capable of reducing light from the speed of 186000 miles per second to a velocity of zero. Then it can be re-directed at will. This unlimited personal power is described as the nearest thing there is to being God.

As with his *UFO* script for 'Timelash', Feely takes many opportunities to demonstrate the power of his antagonist, too. At one point, he takes Koenig's laser, puts it to his own head and fires. The laser bathes his body in light but instead of killing him, it seems to give him strength. He also makes an Eagle vanish into thin air, Maya deducing it is still there, but the molecules are dispersed.

In one of the best moments of the episode, Alan Carter is determined to launch into space in an Eagle, to rescue Koenig, Helena, Tony and Maya from a planet they've been transported to. The wannabe God is seen sweating and shaking as he fights to contain the sheer power of the Eagle, its engines enhanced with added side-boosters, with Alan pouring the power on and on. He succeeds in keeping the Eagle in place, but we see the toll it takes on the super being.

Of course, the idea of a visitor from space claiming to be God, while hardly original, is quite an interesting one. The story improves when we're clear on the idea he's actually an alien. It turns out his real name is Magus, a cosmic magician and someone who has appeared in Earth history and mythology.

Playing the role of Magus is Guy Rolfe, a very good actor who is famous for the movie role of *Sardonicus*. If you don't know about *Sardonicus* and have never seen it, I recommend looking into it, if you like cult movies and classic horror.

Rolfe is not quite in the same league as Peter Cushing and Christopher Lee, but he is definitely a horror legend in his own right and probably an underrated one, deserving of wider recognition.

That being the case, it's nice to see him on *Space:1999* and playing a guest villain.

When Magus first appears, we are treated to some of Feely's lovely, witty dialog. Magus, claiming to be God and the Alphans' creator, says some of his creations are like tame rabbits and would be on their knees or offering up a sacrificial goat.

Koenig remarks, "we're a little low on sacrificial goats." Magus invokes Mankind's propensity for force and aggression to make an impression and causes an Eagle to explode on the launch pad.

The false God soon announces his plan to use the four leads of year two as his new Adams and Eves and transports them to a nearby planet. Another great line of dialog is when the Alphans encounter a force barrier on the planet, walling them into the so-called new Garden of Eden. "Congratulations," says Koenig sarcastically, "you're a big, big physicist!"

Here the episode takes a turn which I can only assume is another contractual obligation owed by the script writer to Fred Freiberger. The price of admission, or for a writer, the price of commission, seems to be the addition of some kind of *Star Trek-*like sub plot with lots of sexual chemistry, kissing etc. Magus, insisting he is God, wants Maya to partner up with Koenig, Tony to partner with Helena.

The point of this situation escapes me, frankly. If the idea was titillation or something similar, I think it really doesn't work out that way. If the idea was to make the viewer feel almost as uncomfortable watching Koenig kiss Maya and Tony kiss Helena as the actors probably felt performing it, then I think it succeeds.

Perhaps this is meant to help us, and the characters feel so annoyed with Magus that we really get invested in seeing him ultimately get defeated. Considering the intention so far this season has been for John and Helena's romantic sub text from season one to be more overt and solid this season and for Tony and Maya to only have eyes for each other, it really does feel a little strange.

The compensation, however, is more great lines. Tony's "you've got a lot to learn about humanity, Santa Claus" is very good, but one of the best lines for my money is when Magus's powers force Koenig to kiss Maya. Just before he gives in and does it, he says to her, "we can't fight City Hall forever."

Once the episode gets this sub plot over and done with, the episode starts to improve considerably. The last twenty minutes or so contains some interesting scenes and moments, such as Magus catching Maya in the form of an owl and not realising it is her, Koenig and Tony fighting off some giant lizard monsters and meeting a mutant who explains the truth about Magus's interest in pair bonding is actually about trying to learn the secret of creating life and finally our heroes deducing the source of his power and coming up with a plan to stop him.

"Superman afraid of the dark?" Tony laughs incredulously, but Koenig's plan is to cut Magus off from his source of power by "being primitive", the one thing he would not expect from these technologically reliant space explorers.

The old, covered pit trick is well used here and I am going to assume the Alphans found the pit, rather than digging it with their bare hands. Koenig cleverly goads Magus by attacking his ego. Magus's pride gets him to step into the pit and down he goes into the darkness, defeating the light-dependent alien, quicker than you can say *Guy Rolfe's stunt double.*

Once the pit is covered and the light is cut off, Magus is unable to protect the planet from the gravity of the passing Moon. This has a catastrophic affect and Brian Johnson goes into overdrive with the effects as the planet rips open and starts to explode into pieces. While it is brief, it compares relatively well with the similar storm and chaos scenes in the finale of season one's 'Matter of Life and Death'. Our heroes blast off in the nick of time and the whole planet explodes. All of this is really well done.

In fact, with the possible exception of the mutant's costume, which conceals a very good guest actor, Bernard Kay, the whole episode is nicely produced and directed with skill and style. Maya does get a couple of transformations in, but this is generally an episode about a humanoid alien and offers a solidly scripted plotline.

As much as the forced romance sub plot feels like a bad idea and not particularly likely to appeal to anyone, 'New Adam, New Eve' is mostly a good, solid episode which is worth persevering with.

Apparently, this script was so easy for the production team to work with, it led to Fred Frieberger deciding to commission Terrence Feely's second storyline, The 'Bringers of Wonder'. And for that, I am truly grateful.

MAYA'S COMPUTER

ANALYSIS

7/10

A tight script which probably should have been better than the end result. A great guest star makes it worth a look, too. It's all very *Star Trek*-like, but this is not really a problem.

CATACOMBS OF THE MOON

'Catacombs of the Moon' is such an atypical episode for year two that we have to wonder how on Earth it was smuggled past Fred Frieberger without him objecting overwhelmingly to it being made. 'Catacombs' is written by a returning season one scriptwriter and deals with the Moon on a 'Collision Course' with a mysterious phenomenon in space which generates immense heat and threatens to burn up Moon Base Alpha. But the cloud may contain some kind of cosmic intelligence and it may also be in telepathic communication, albeit unconsciously, with a member of the Moon Base Alpha crew.

The Alphan in question is highly religious and believes that survival is a question of faith, not science. Patrick sees visions of Alpha consumed and destroyed by flame. Patrick's surrealistic visions involve him running in slow motion, but unable to get through a ring of fire, which surrounds an old-fashioned four-poster bed containing his dying wife, who has her arms outreached towards him. A truly bizarre thing is that this vision is visualised as being on the surface of the Moon.

The subplot of the episode involves Helena and Dr Ben Vincent struggling to come up with a functioning artificial heart which can be transplanted into Pat's dying wife to save her from death.

I can only think that maybe the writer sold this plotline about Alpha getting hotter and hotter by saying the increase of temperature on the base would cause the ladies to start walking around dressed in bikinis and swimsuits and Tony would be in a tank top and this might add some sex appeal to the show.

The episode is not without its flaws. The Commander's decision to take off and go on an exploratory trip ahead to investigate the fiery space phenomenon is something which happens off screen and is suggested by an additional voice-over from Dr Russell. Things like this feel like cutting corners in the production and it detracts slightly from the effectiveness of the finished episode. Helena is not overly effective at conveying her speculation about the possible intelligence within the fiery space inferno and its effect on the troubled mind of Patrick.

However, while it certainly would have worked better in season one than it does as a season two episode, 'Catacombs' is an interesting, even somewhat haunting tale of faith and catastrophe and the threats posed by a mysterious and dangerous Universe to human survival. It is a genuinely intelligent and remarkable episode.

MAYA'S COMPUTER

ANALYSIS

7/10

Needs more of Koenig, but this is a very interesting story all the same. Patrick is hard to sympathise with due to his cynicism and fanaticism, and his poor sick wife doesn't get enough dialog, but the whole thing feels enjoyably reminiscent of the more ethereal year one stories, albeit a little less than fully realized. Imperfect, in execution, but well worth a close look.

THE AB CHRYSALIS

'The AB Chrysalis' is the second story from Tony Barwick, and it is a much better story than his first contribution to this season and not just because this time around there is no dance sequence. This is easily one of the best episodes in the first two thirds of the season.

What's interesting about the plot is that it is very similar to the type of story the series did regularly in season one, featuring the Moon on a 'Collision Course' in space.

It also could easily have been expanded into a two-part story and, in fact, it would have been even better if they had done so. The first 10 minutes of the episode deals with the moon on a 'Collision Course' with dangerous space phenomena, a situation which has been apparently happening for quite some time before the beginning of the narrative.

This part of the story could have easily been expanded into the first half of a two-part storyline and would have been similar to many first season episodes such as 'Black Sun' and 'Space Brain' where we see the people of Alpha struggle with the fact they are headed for an imminent collision and probable destruction in space.

Possibly we could have begun with the Alphans discovering the threat when a pair of Eagles are out in space. One of them could have been destroyed by the energy shock waves and another, perhaps piloted by Alan, could have been damaged and sent out of control.

As the Moon continued to drift towards the vicinity of the threat, Alpha may have been damaged and possibly the Commander could have suffered some injury, leaving him spending a short stint in the Medical Centre, until he recovered.

The final act of part one could have been the first 10 minutes which we see in the episode as it is, with Koenig, Alan and Maya setting off to find answers before time runs out.

This would have left part two free to be completely dedicated to the journey undertaken by the Alphan trio to reach the alien star system and confront the aliens who are behind the threat. It's a great pity such a strong idea was confined to a single episode format, but as it stands, it is still a pretty strong entry for the series.

As always with his writing, Tony Barwick gives us a very good story structure with good pacing and plenty of interest to engage our attention. The episode immediately draws us into a situation and hooks us into the plight of the Alphans.

One point of interest in the episode is the appearance of guest star Sarah Douglas just a few years before she became famous as one of the three escaped prisoners from the planet Krypton in

Superman 2, where she joined General Zod in terrorising the Earth.

The threat to Alpha turns out to be a defensive system set up by an alien race of people who just want to be left alone to do their own thing. Part of the interest of the story is that the Alphans have to go through a lengthy process to reach and communicate with the aliens, contacting them through things such as a computer system which protects the local people on the alien planet.

One of the most interesting aspects is that the computer on the planet uses probes which take the form of bouncing white spheres. These bouncing balls roll along corridors into rooms and hop up onto tall pedestals, where they pulsate with light and talk to the visitors from Earth.

It was assumed by many fans of Anderson shows that they were also the inspiration for the similar Zeroids in Gerry Anderson's 1980s series *Terra Hawks*. However, when asked point-blank about this notion in his final interview in the late 1980s, Barwick said this was not the case, so it was simply a case of coincidence.

The episode generates some tense drama when Alan is trapped in a room full of chlorine gas by his own desperation to save Alpha. Maya has to transform in order to rescue him, becoming a chlorine breathing alien which would appear again in the episode 'The Beta Cloud'.

There are some interesting lines of dialogue near the finale of the episode as the Commander challenges the aliens and their idealistic concepts of advancement through biological development. They claim they are seeking to reach a level of perfection through logical progression in their life cycle of birth and rebirth.

However, Koenig puts it to them that they should save his base and his people because creation is the better choice than destruction.

Barwick characterises John Koenig very well with this dialogue. He also builds up the idea that this really could be the final curtain and the end for the people of Moon Base Alpha.

Koenig speaks his tearful final commendation to all the people of the Alpha base for their fortitude and courage since the Moon left Earth orbit. This is another reason why the episode would have made a very good two-part story. The script tries very hard to create a sense that this could really be the end of the journey.

If there is one negative point to the episode, it is probably the rather strange notion that one of the aliens has some kind of romantic fascination with the Commander. This feels like yet another case of something the writer was asked to add to the story in order to get commissioned to write the episode, probably by Fred Freiberger.

It feels like a way of saying this series has something in common with *Star Trek*, once again. Perhaps wisely, the writer Barwick simply uses it to make one of the aliens annoyed enough to want to not cooperate in saving the Moon Base from destruction, dismissing her fellow alien's fascination with Koenig as obvious and stupid.

Of course, there is a happy ending, ultimately, but this is well handled as it feels like Koenig's words about creation, hope and loyalty have resonated with the aliens and paid off for them, with the aliens helping Koenig and his friends on their journey home.

Alan and Maya repeat the Commander's words back to him as if to acknowledge that he was right to say what he said. Koenig grins happily and tells Helena over the video link "we're coming home."

Again, this is a nice call back, embellishing the notion floated in the first season, notably at the end of the 'Black Sun' episode, that Alpha is now more than just a Moon Base to these people. It has become a home to these wandering Earth people, their home among the stars.

All in all, this is one of the few truly great episodes in the first two thirds of the second season, a real stand out, and should not be missed.

MAYA'S COMPUTER

ANALYSIS

9/10

This one is a real gem of the second season. Exciting, suspenseful and intriguing with a dangerous journey for our heroes as they struggle to save Alpha from destruction. Their efforts to establish communication with the enigmatic alien threat and the tense ending all add up to a gripping episode. The cosmic scale of the action is great too, very like year one at its epic best. Not to be missed.

SEED OF DESTRUCTION

Fans of Martin Landau's considerable acting ability should find much to enjoy and appreciate in this episode. It ranks along with 'The Lambda Factor' and 'Bringers of Wonder' for being a showcase of Landau's range as an actor.

Unlike the hysteria and paranoia of Bringers and the emotional breakdown of Lambda Factor, this one is unique for allowing Landau to do something he has often done very well, bring out the evil and menacing side.

When Koenig is knocked out and replaced by his reflection, Landau has the opportunity to create a sinister alternative Koenig who is like nothing we've seen before.

The first season of *1999* had plenty of surrealism but in the more straight forward second season it is far less common. So, there is something refreshing about the bizarre way in which the Commander takes a spooky walk through a hall of mirrors on an alien asteroid only to be stalked by his own reflection which simply steps right out of the mirror.

Landau initially plays the reflection with a smile like a hungry cat, predatory and preying upon the humans. But when he returns to Alpha with Alan, the reflection puts his plan into action, drawing the resistance of Maya. Here Landau shows the calm facade cracking, and the authoritarian starts to emerge.

The situation allows the rest of the cast to bring some good acting to the story as they wrestle with the apparent changes which have come over their friend. But good as Schell, Tate, Bain and Merton are here, this is Landau's show all the way. Having said that Tony Anholt is very funny when he gets worked up and suddenly realises it and says, "I'm talking like I've been drinking my own beer!"

On the other hand, "my being head of security is a joke" could be his most unfortunate line ever.

Maya's role here is focused on her scientific abilities and she is seen tackling the situation as a researcher, but we do get a couple of brief transformations. One of these is interesting because she impersonates another Alphan to get past the watching eyes of the reflection.

Landau starts to bring a cold inhuman quality to the fore when Helena confronts him about the change she's noticed. Bain is great here. Her shock and muted but growing horror is really good as she realises Koenig is not Koenig.

But when Tony and Maya defy the reflection and take off in an Eagle, Landau really escalates the reflection's tyranny and authoritarian persona to a grotesque and unnerving level.

Tate and Merton are superb as they try to stop the monstrous reflection from shooting down the Eagle. Suddenly, the reflection shifts his tactics and Landau brings us the Mr Reasonable version, a mercurial shift to manipulation. The way he puts it to Helena that he could use his authority to have her confined if she continues to speak against him is very well written and played.

The performance hits its biggest peak when the real Commander arrives back in time to expose the reflection in front of everyone. Rather than taking the arrival of the real deal as a defeat the reflection goes all out, trying every lie and deflection it can come up with to make the Alphans hesitate a little longer, to buy time for its energy stealing plan. Finally caught out by the one thing it can't disguise, the part in Koenig's hair, the reflection becomes a mad eyed, laughing psycho. This is perhaps a little over the top and not a great approach but in the circumstances it's fair to say Landau needed to give it something big for the ending and he definitely pulls out the stops.

The destruction of the reflection with sound waves is suitably surreal again, using a superimposed mirror which shatters and the revelation that the whole thing was just a lump of green crystal.

The episode ends without any attempts at humour, another good thing about it, lending it a haunting final moment for a change.

All in all, this is one of the very best season two episodes, certainly compared to the majority of the first two thirds of the series. It's a great showcase for Landau's acting chops and has a nice touch of spooky weirdness not unlike shows such as *Twilight Zone* or *Sapphire and Steel*. More in this vein would've been very welcome and might have helped the series cement a good name for itself.

MAYA'S COMPUTER

ANALYSIS

9/10

A surreal story with lots of weirdness, halls of mirrors, spooky voices, the doppelgänger trope well visualized and a great building of suspense. Best of all, there is plenty of great acting from Martin Landau, who reminds us that he was not only a great leading man, but a terrific crazy, evil baddie when given a chance.

THE BETA CLOUD

A hairy monster arrives on the Moon to tear Alpha to bits in search of the life support system. And it's Dave Prowse in his prime playing the monster.

Let's face it, this is probably the most re-watchable episode of the second season and one of the most fun things ever! It's also the closest Tony and Bill Fraser got to looking like *Starsky and Hutch* on Moon Base Alpha. Or do I mean Bodie and Doyle? Sometimes the fun end of science fiction is more enjoyable than all the navel-gazing intellectual stuff could ever be. 'The Beta Cloud' is sheer kinetic fun.

The episode kicks off with the arrival of the titular cloud and an outbreak of fainting spells and dizziness all over Moon Base Alpha which may or may not be connected to the cloud. Since no link between the cloud and the fainting and weakness stuff is ever established, it seems more likely this is purely McGuffin from writer Fred Freiberger, and he soon forgets all about it. However, the story makes more sense if we assume the cloud is radiating some sort of rays which are causing most of the Alphans to pass out.

Koenig and Helena are both soon bed-ridden, leaving this episode to become a showcase for the double act of Tony and Maya, but leaving plenty of room for Bill Fraser, Sandra, and Alan Carter to get in on the action, or at least the acting. This is one of the things which makes the episode special, it's a chance for cast members other than Landau and Bain to carry the show.

The main guest star here is David Prowse, just shy of landing his most famous role as Darth Vader in 1977's *Star Wars*, when it was actually just called *Star Wars*. But before he donned Darth's helmet, he has to endure a baptism of fire on Moon Base Alpha that involves plenty of pyrotechnics and a fire extinguisher in the groin for good measure.

Fans of Tony and Maya will love their tense moment in the finale where Tony confesses his love for her with the words 'Psychon's my favorite planet.'

Alan Carter and Sandra do a great job and once again get plenty more to do than their usual type of roles allow.

John Hugg is loads of fun as Bill Fraser here, accidentally 'testing' the electrical barrier by bumping into it and hurling himself into action against the monster.

The monster does look rather fake but for once that's okay because it is a fake. It's a robot in disguise. Possibly an alien infiltration weapon, the monster that is actually a machine takes the show into *Doctor Who* territory, reminiscent of the robot Yeti.

If nothing else, I always have fun watching this one because when Tony asks, "where's Graham?"

the monster opens its mouth in silence and my wife always shouts, "I ate him!" in her best monstrous voice.

MAYA'S COMPUTER

ANALYSIS

9/10

It could be argued that this one is silly nonsense, and unintentionally funny, but it's a wild ride directed with style and verve and the whole episode is way too much fun to dislike. Dave Prowse takes one for the team as the robot monster and Maya saves Alpha with her cleverness and amazing powers.

SPACE WARP

And so, we come to Fred Frieberger's 'Space Warp'. How do you make an episode without Maya? By making an episode that is all about Maya. And that's because Maya can change into other things.

So, with Catherine Schell only available to film a few quick scenes of herself in bed, so she can be free to shoot a separate episode elsewhere, this episode focuses on Maya constantly changing shape from one creature to another.

One of the interesting things about having an alien on Moon Base Alpha such as Maya is that the character is slightly ambiguous.

Some of the details about the limitations and potential of Maya's powers of shape shifting seem to change in different episodes. For example, in the first action-adventure episode written by the season's new producer the 'Rules of Luton', Maya is trapped while caged in the form of a bird. She is not able to simply transform into another shape, such as a small flying insect and fly out of the cage and escape. We are also told that she can only hold that form for one hour.

Later in the series, however, we are told she can hold a form for three hours.

In this episode Maya seems to be very capable of changing form from one type of creature to another and then another. This suggests perhaps that Maya is getting better at her mastery of molecular transformation as time goes by. She can hold the form longer and she can perform ongoing transformations from form to form. Actress Catherine Schell is almost universally praised for her charming performance as Maya and while there is certainly nothing wrong with the idea of her going for the alpha Scream Queen title it has to be said that her wild-eyed screaming at the camera before she loses molecular control in the early stage of this episode is a little hard on the ear drums.

In production terms 'Space Warp' is an episode which is very much a game of two halves. On the one hand the model work and visual effects depicting the moon going through a space time warp and being catapulted several light-years across space as well as the derelict alien spaceship and an out-of-control Eagle which is flipped by the feverish Maya in the underground Eagle hanger are absolutely spectacular and exceptionally well done for the period in which the show was produced. On the other hand, the monsters Maya transforms into are easily the worst scene in season two and probably the whole of *Space: 1999* the first alien she transforms into is not terrible, but it does look a bit cheap and unconvincing.

The second alien monster she turns into looks absolutely dreadful. It is clearly the creature from the episode 'The Beta Cloud' thinly disguised with an added layer of hair and fur. This thing really looks awful. When it goes running across the lunar surface in the finale of the episode and fights the pursuing Alan and Helena things really start to come unstuck. Alan's helmet visor opens during the fight with a monster which only serves to add insult to injury.

And then there's the captain of the derelict alien spaceship who appears on screen in video recording is viewed by Koenig and Tony. With his ill-fitting and badly designed pink Perspex space helmet, the alien who is inexplicably credited as Grasshopper, looks terrible and probably was a very uncomfortable fit for the actor playing the part.

These bad points are a real pity because the whole episode is a real popcorn movie and an action-packed ride from start to finish. It is all directed with great skill and flair by Peter Medak who uses many great camera angles and plenty of dynamic and energetic fight sequences to bring this story to rollicking action packed life.

Although the episode definitely has its flaws, there are many good points here to enjoy. If you can turn a blind eye to the dodgy looking aliens, then one of the nice things here is that Alan Carter gets to be the Commander of Moon Base Alpha in John's absence and Nick Tate does a very good job running the base as Alan Carter. There is a power failure caused by damage from Alpha going through the space or so the lights go down low giving Command Center an added layer of atmosphere.

Another good point of the episode is that the recorded messages from the dead alien captain on the derelict included a lengthy monologue which is actually quite well written and very detailed telling the story of how the aliens met a grim fate but left behind the clues Koenig and Tony need to find their way back through the space warp and reunite themselves with Moon Base Alpha.

There is also a very strong focus on astronaut procedural drama in the sequences in which John and Tony try to work out how to get through the space warp and back to Moon Base Alpha. All in all, 'Space Warp' is not a particularly good episode and is not intellectual in any way, shape, or form. But it does contain some of the space procedural drama which *Space: 1999* is known and loved for some brilliant visual effects and some well-directed action.

It is the kind of colourful and fast paced episode which one can sit and watch as pure popcorn movie sci-fi fun and adventure. However, it should be noted that it was part of the *Cosmic Princess* compilation movie which was lampooned by *Mystery Science Theatre 3000* and that is quite an indictment. In certain respects, this is the worst episode of the season, but it is certainly far from being the least entertaining. And that Eagle crash is really an outstanding piece of work from special effects genius Brian Johnson, so it's definitely worth watching with a big bowl of popcorn and a forgiving attitude. You can't say fairer than that.

MAYA'S COMPUTER

ANALYSIS

8/10

Flawed but like 'Beta Cloud', it is fun all the way. The pace and energy are enjoyable, the stunt team get a workout, there's some proper astronaut procedural work for Koenig and Tony and the model work is once again a highlight with the brilliant Eagle crash in the underground hangar as a cherry on top of the cake.

A MATTER OF BALANCE

'A Matter of Balance' is another script which was met by initial concern and disdain from Martin Landau. In this case, he was probably rather more justified in his concerns. But it's not all bad, by any means.

The story is written by Pip and Jane Baker, a husband-and-wife team, who had previously written additional material for the movie version of *The Night of the Big Heat* and would go on to become contributors to *Doctor Who* in the 1980s, creating Time Lady villainess The Rani.

In *Doctor Who* fandom, Pip and Jane Baker have a somewhat poor reputation, due in part to some odd notions in their scripts and some overly complex or strange-sounding dialog.

However, their reputation is possibly a little unfair. The Bakers had good points which were not always obvious to the audience. Television scripts often go through a lot of rewrites and changes and often take a long time to get written, often requiring deadline extensions. The Bakers, however, had a reputation behind the scenes as consummate professionals who could be depended upon to deliver a shootable script, one which did not require much in the way of changes or rewrites and deliver it on time.

They also had a good grasp of formats and characters, which meant they often gave all the main characters plenty of story involvement and plenty to do over the course of the story. They would never side line a main character in his own show, for example, something which was apparently discussed around their time starting on *Doctor Who* as a concern of the lead actor.

A famous incident in *Doctor Who* was when a writer passed away mid-way through writing a two-part story and Pip and Jane were asked to write part two with no idea what the writer had intended.

Apparently, their wrap up segment was delivered in an extremely short amount of time, only a day or two, and was able to go before the cameras to complete the story. As dependable professionals, the Bakers were well liked and respected.

Their *Space:1999* episode is well paced, nicely structured and engaging in the telling. The end results are a generally quality production, too, with nice direction and effects. Perhaps the script starts to get into trouble when it comes to the Bakers' notions of anti-matter and the plight of the anti-matter aliens. The script gets into some very tongue-twisting dialogue when Koenig has to verbalise the idea that the aliens are projecting into their minds the illusion that an anti-matter being is solid. This may be the point where Landau felt a little unhappy!

It's hard to discuss this episode without mentioning a couple of other points, Shermeen and Vindrus.

Lynne Frederick, who plays Shermeen, was a remarkable young woman, known for her striking beauty and the winner of a type of most promising new talent award for her acting skills. After her career started to take off, she fell under the spell of the gifted but infamous Peter Sellers.

Sellers has been described by other women in his life as a manic-depressive and someone with no redeeming features, among other things. After her husband's passing, Lynne became the target of criticism from people who felt that she was a bad person when she inherited Sellers' estate and was labelled a gold digger.

However, it seems a little unlikely, to me, that it was her, rather than Peter Sellers, who was the source of the issues. It's far more likely that she was simply sympathetic to her husband's point of view and as an impressionable young woman believed his side of the story when it came to the conflicts Peter Sellers had been entrenched in with the various people in his life, including his children from a previous marriage.

Lynne's career was killed by the controversy surrounding Sellers. She slowly vanished from the limelight and died at age 39.

The story is tragic yet the few performances we have to judge her by reveal that she was both vibrant and gifted and she definitely is the highlight of her *Space: 1999* episode, bringing a remarkable presence to her character. Just for the chance to see this often-overlooked artist in action, the episode is well worth watching.

Stuart Wilson also makes a lasting impression as the main villain of the story. His costume eclipses that of the alien villain in season one's 'Alpha Child' episode for most outrageous male costume. Despite this or perhaps partly because of this, he and his character remain popular with fans of the series.

The ghostly manifestation effects are remarkable and look very convincing most of the time. When the writers Pip and Jane Baker wrote their first *Doctor Who* script for Colin Baker a few years later, the Doctor finds himself strung up between a pair of trees and as he is trying to get down, he remarks it's only a matter of balance.

The Bakers were fascinated with botany and so Shermeen creates a mutation of a plant which attacks crew man Eddie Collins.

It is probably just as well they weren't obsessed with ornithology or Eddie may have been devoured by giant sparrow.

The monster known as the Thaed is the same costume from 'Beta Cloud' and 'Space Warp' dressed up with spines and a new costume for the body parts.

Despite this the results are very impressive. In fact, it is probably the best the monster costume looks in any of its appearances in the season. All in all, this is a stylish and well-made episode which entertains despite the fact it doesn't all make complete sense.

The special effects department delivers a very neat moment at the end of the episode when the entire planet vanishes from under the Eagles, leaving them suspended in space.

Very cool work from Brian Johnson and his team once again.

MAYA'S COMPUTER

ANALYSIS

6/10

Silly but passable nonsense, elevated by two very fine guest stars and some nice production. The location work is particularly nice, and the model work intercuts with the live action very well, notably at the end.

BRINGERS OF WONDER
PART ONE AND TWO

Koenig loses his mind and crashes his Eagle into a nuclear waste dome. As he rests in Medical Center, a spaceship arrives from Earth, bringing old friends to take them home. He recovers to learn the friends from Earth are hostile aliens out to destroy Alpha.

Koenig races against time to save Alpha from total annihilation and all that stands in his way is his own people.

When I first saw 'Bringers of Wonder', I was in high school. My reaction to the first appearance of the creatures was pretty strong. Decades later, I got the DVDs and played it to my wife. When the creatures were revealed, she went "Ewwwww! Yuck!!! Oh, my God!!! They're HORRIBLE!!!"

The one huge eye, the quivering, the blood flowing through transparent veins on the exterior of the body, the dripping green slime...when they are revealed suddenly to a new viewer, there's a visceral sense of repulsion. And then the one who practically climbs on top of Koenig and presses down over his face, to suffocate him in the cliff-hanger, ending in a silent, frozen scream, that totally nails the horror for me.

The monsters seemed very well conceived and executed and best of all, the camera shots and editing were "in your face", like they were pushing for these things to shock the Hell out of the audience.

There was none of the punch-pulling or aiming for a family audience of previous episodes, it felt instead like there was no coziness intended, that these things were an attempt to really horrify.

Like the best of classic *Doctor Who*, these aliens are proper behind-the-sofa creatures when they first show up and in their moments of slowly creeping and slithering toward an intended victim, such as the helpless Keonig in episode one and the hapless Maya, trapped inside the shape of one of them and trying desperately to revert back to her true self in episode two.

The narrative of 'Bringers of Wonder' is a real winner. It taps into some really strong material and it's the type of material that made *Space:1999* popular in the first place, something not always true of season two stories.

For a start, there's hideous, slimy, rubbery, quivering, decidedly non-humanoid monsters with one big eye who make a very sudden and shocking first appearance and also pose a merciless physical threat to one of the main good guys in the first episode. Where have we seen that before? Well, the shocking first appearance of the one-eyed monster in 'Dragon's Domain' comes to mind, along with the way it tries to drag Tony Cellini to his doom.

Then there's the fact the Alphans have all their minds manipulated and become happy and cheerful but turn decidedly nasty against Commander Koenig once they realise he is the one man not affected. It's the kind of paranoid, everyone is out to get our hero, mind-control science fiction drama we all know and love from 'The Guardian of Piri', right down to Helena knocking Koenig out and confining him to Medical Center.

Then we have the threat of nuclear waste stored on the Moon, astronauts fighting each other on the lunar surface and the possibility all life on the Moon will be wiped out by a huge nuclear explosion. This is a direct call back to 'Breakaway' and the crazed astronauts, the massive nuclear explosion and the very beginning of Alpha's odyssey.

Best of all, it's tapping into the idea of the Alphans as lost people, cut off from home, longing for Earth. It's all very well to talk of home, but 'Bringers of Wonder' actually allows us to meet the people, the friends, family, mentors, lovers and siblings, which the people of Alpha left behind when the breakaway separation event took place.

Terrence Feely weaves these elements together seamlessly into a genuinely clever and suspenseful narrative, which never feels derivative or lazy. He presents them intelligently, with wit, suspense and moments of real pathos. There's a philosophical ending, too, with the whole notion of life, meaning and fulfilment laid out in front of Koenig as he sees Bartlett reduced to a blissful, impotent zombie.

The cast excel themselves here, too, with Landau on particularly strong dramatic form. And Nick Tate deserves special mention for his wild-eyed, alien-controlled performance in the climax where he tries to kill Koenig and then attempts to plug the nuclear fuel canister into the atomic core and blow Alpha to kingdom come.

The guest cast are all very good. Nicholas Young from *The Tomorrow People* had considerable experience playing a telepath by this point in his career and he is very good here conveying the strangeness of the aliens in their human guise.

Director Tom Clegg really does a great job too. The whole story has pace and energy and real suspense. Those one-eyed aliens look extra real in the gloomy shots, glowing and pulsating in the darkened Medical Centre.

The slow-motion scenes on the lunar surface in episode two makes the aliens look like jellyfish under the sea, the way they seem to ripple and pulsate. Part two is notable for featuring more lunar surface scenes than just about any other episode in season two and really reminds us that this is a show about a base on the Moon. The casting of Stuart Damon as Tony's brother is inspired, too, as they look as if they genuinely could be brothers in real life.

'Bringers of Wonder' is so good, it really makes me wish the production team had attempted a few more two-part stories to really drag the audience in and I wish this had been shown very early in the season, to help win viewers to the show's new look and style.

'Bringers of Wonder' was also chosen to be the first compilation movie release of *Space:1999*, under the title *Destination: Moon Base Alpha*. Despite an opening scrawl which begins 'far out into the galaxy of the Universe is the Moon.', which is enough to make anyone who has a basic idea of astronomy do a double take, Destination works really well as a movie, particularly if you're familiar with the series. In the dark days when *Space:1999* was off the air and had yet to be released in its true format, *Destination* was the only *Space:1999* available on home video. I hired it several times from my local video store in those days, happy to keep spending my money for a chance to get a fix of Moon Base Alpha.

And while there is no evidence *Destination* was a big money spinner for the owners, two subsequent movie compilations were released using season one episodes, and another featuring 'Metamorph' and 'Space Warp'. So, I guess it must have made at least some profit for ITC.

All in all, 'Bringers of Wonder' is a remarkable achievement and were it not sacrilege to name a year two story above the best of year 1, I might be tempted to call it my favourite *Space:1999* story of them all.

All in all, this is season two's best.

"It's better to live as your own man than as a fool in someone else's dream." (Commander John Koenig.)

MAYA'S COMPUTER

ANALYSIS

10/10

Pure excitement and enjoyment. A great story, great and truly horrid alien monsters and great material for the regulars. Epic stuff which is enough to draw you in and get you involved, holding your attention right to the very end. A classic adventure which probably could have served as year two's calling card.

'THE LAMBDA FACTOR'

Alpha becomes affected by a force which turns many Alphans into temporary psychics. Koenig becomes haunted by the ghosts of his past.

This is the one and only contribution to the series by *Doctor Who* script editor, writer and noveliser Terrance Dicks, one of the most well regarded and well-loved people associated with *Doctor Who*.

Why is his presence as a writer on *Space:1999* such a big deal? To answer this question, it is important to understand the background of *Doctor Who* and what exactly Terrance Dicks did there.

Then we might better appreciate what he brings to the table on *Space:1999*.

Science Fiction began in earnest on television in the UK with the three *Quatermass* serials of Nigel Kneale of the 1950s. These tales were six-week serialised stories written by the remarkable television pioneer Nigel Kneale. They focused on Professor Bernard *Quatermass*, of British Experimental Rocket Group or BERG. I have noted that *Space:1999*'s Professor Bergman seems to have been inspired by the Professor from Kneale's three magnum opuses. Gerry and Sylvia Anderson certainly drew a lot of inspiration from *Quatermass* when they made *UFO*, the series out of which *Space:1999* evolved and developed. A lot of the imagery and ideas in *Quatermass* are revived in such early *Space:1999* episodes as 'Force of Life' and 'Space Brain'.

But *Quatermass* was also the beginning of what became *Doctor Who*. The Pertwee era in particular was an attempt to bring *Doctor Who* down to modern day Earth and reinvent the Doctor as a sort of continuation of *Quatermass* and it is the Pertwee era where Terrance Dicks worked as script editor alongside Producer Barry Letts.

After their time on *Doctor Who* ended, Letts and Dicks went on to make a six-episode series called *Moon Base 3*, which was set in a small lunar base in the near future. This series was a very realistic dramatisation of life on a moon colony and dealt with the psychological and emotional issues of humans living and working on the Moon. Dicks later expressed his regrets about the series, feeling it was overdone in the grim and gritty realism department and even responded to a question about the show by calling it a failure. There was an early episode called 'Behemoth' in which a monster seems to be the menace, but the monster turns out to have a much more psychological explanation.

The impression Terrance Dicks gave was that if he had been free to change *Moon Base 3*, he might have gone in a more imaginative, adventurous direction. It is highly possibly, therefore, to assume 'The Lambda Factor' is just the type of thing he would have liked to write for *Moon Base 3*, were he free to go in a more imaginative direction.

The theme of the episode is classic Terrance Dicks. Ghosts and horror are the main focus, something very in keeping with the influences which arose in *Doctor Who* during and immediately after his tenure on that series. It strikes me that a lot of *Space:1999* seems more about the supernatural than science fiction, despite the high-tech setting and this goes right back to the beginning of the first season. So, Terrance's decision to build a story around horror and supernatural ideas seems fitting and very welcome in the second season, since the second year of *Space:1999* is often purer in its space opera narratives.

Some of the first season episodes actually seemed to be ghost stories and tales of evil, vengeful or sad and longing spirits, rather than aliens. Alpha's Universe in the beginning seemed to be dream-like and defiant of science and logic at times. This seems to be strongly born out when watching episodes written by Johnny Byrne. (Possibly my favorite writer on season one).

As a long-time fan of the show, pondering these notions, I once had a bizarre thought about the first series of *Space:1999*, that perhaps the Alphans all died in the nuclear explosion in episode 1 and they are ghosts in heaven, now, drifting around, meeting God and Helena's dead husband, encountering evil spirits, Ernst Queller facing judgement and having to redeem himself for his sins, etc.

Someone told me years ago that Gerry Anderson loved episodes where it was all a dream ('Attack on

Cloudbase' and *UFO*'s 'Ordeal' being two famous or infamous examples) and I sometimes think season one of *1999* is a whole series where it's almost like a dream. 'Missing Link', in fact, seems to challenge us with Koenig waking up at the end in hospital...was the plot with Raan of Zenno real, or a dream?

I guess when it's like a dream, you become an armchair Freud and ask what the dream meant. Foster's fear of alien abduction on *UFO*, I suppose. But Johnny Byrne was a poet, so was *1999* allegorical, was it metaphor? Is Terra Nova the paradise that represents the life Helena and Lee had together, but she has to accept she's lost it and him, watching the planet out the window as they drift away from it at the end? 'Another Time, Another Place' is dream-like...a possible future for themselves...Paul and Sandra watch the Sun setting, their last sunset, as their hopes of a new life and love evaporate.

Again, the plot logic and science are often scant, or left to us to work out for ourselves, but as metaphor, it seems to carry some meaning. This is what gets me about the negative critics and naysayers who attacked *Space:1999*.

As much as I can see it is a show that many find easy to criticise, there's something in it which seems to haunt me. David Tomblin produced *The Prisoner*, which was very surreal, and he was given carte blanche on *UFO* to make it more surreal and he directed for *1999* as well. I've always felt that the Anderson series begin the way the previous series ended. The surreal nature of later *UFO* carries into early *Space: 1999*. Both 'Timelash' on *UFO* and 'Missing Link' on *1999* end with the Commander in bed and we can wonder if his adventure was a weird dream in both cases.

So where does Terrance Dicks fit into this situation? The story does, according to interviews given by Dicks himself, that Fred Freiberger wanted a lot of American writers on *Space:1999*'s second season and this was only agreed to by the unions in the UK on the condition that he also give many jobs to local writers as well. This led to Terrance Dicks being sent along to see Fred by his agent. Fred apparently met with Terrance and told him if he comes up with an idea for an episode he should call. Terrance being the creative man he was had an idea. He wanted to write a story about the Moon Base being haunted and more specifically, a story about Landau's Commander Koenig being haunted.

He apparently phoned Fred, told him the story idea and Fred replied they had a deal. The story also goes that Dicks wrote it, submitted the script, was paid handsomely and never heard a word again. Years later, never having known if his script was actually used, he was surprised to see the episode and was further surprised that the *Space:1999* production team had made it virtually exactly as he had written it, with no noticeable changes or alterations (which is uncommon in television).

Terrance Dicks script gives us an episode where the ghosts are from the Commander's own guilty conscience, and it is an external, alien power in space causing their manifestation. As with his work on *Doctor Who*, there is a clear explanation instead of ambiguity. Lambda waves, emanating from a weird swirling space phenomenon, is afflicting the Alpha crew and awakening dormant centers of the brain, areas of the brain associated with psychic powers.

Dicks makes this episode a cracker by demonstrating his mastery of characterisation and dialogue, something he had to rely on more than special effects in the low budget world of BBC science fiction.

The episode is notable for taking things to a more adult level than he could on *Doctor Who*, too. On *Doctor Who*, Dicks always seemed to give the characters very clearly defined roles, such as military leader, scientist, sidekick/maiden in distress, evil villain, etc. It's perhaps not so strange then to note we see Tony Verdeschi in his role as Head of Security on the Moon Base actually investigating a murder, questioning suspects and checking up on people, not to mention breaking up a brawl between two Alphans who have a falling out. Many other episodes give lip service to his role, but he often seems to be a second to Koenig, running Alpha when the Commander is away or sick. In this script, however, we see he has a job, and he cares about it, too.

Alan Carter's role as chief Eagle pilot is well defined here, too, as he talks to engineer Garforth about problems with Eagle engines. What's more, Terrance puts the audience's favorite Aussie character into a situation of extreme peril.

Helena is well served too, doing tests and medical research. Maya's science role is also involved, not just her shape-shifting powers. In the space of just one episode, Terrance Dicks does a huge amount to define and deepen our grasp of the regulars and the Alphans in general. The script uses the guest cast to make it plain the people of Alpha have romances, marriages and break ups, as well as recreational habits and interests.

But best of all is the way the script delivers great material to the star of the show, Martin Landau. Year two of *Space:1999* has given Landau a number of chances to really display his range and ability as a serious dramatic actor, his tyrannical and conniving twin in 'Seed of Destruction' being one example, his struggling, paranoid, desperately driven performance in 'Bringers of Wonder' being another. But this episode is the icing on the cake for fans of Landau's acting chops.

Faced with the ghosts of his own past and his feelings of guilt about what happened to his friends when he was a young astronaut cadet, Commander John Koenig has an emotional breakdown.

The sight of this strong leader crumbling before our very eyes is shocking and unsettling to behold.

This was a time when men in film and television were often still portrayed as quite tough, even stoic, heroes, somewhere between James Bond and John Wayne.

But as the ghosts of his dead friends appear, like dead Banquo before the eyes of Macbeth, John Koenig runs to his room to hide, before Helena helps him find the courage to face his own fear and guilt. As he stares at them, Helena acting her role of base doctor in a way rarely seen before, Koenig falls apart. His delivery when he tells his dead friends he loves them is enough to break your heart.

This script allows Martin Landau the chance to deliver his best performance in the whole of season two and one of the best performances ever given by a lead actor on television. There's a secondary plotline about Caroline Powell, an Alphan whose powers corrupt her. Her story arc in the episode appears to be influenced by the Stephen King story *Carrie*, which had been adapted into a hugely effective and popular movie in the early 70s. In her defeat, she loses her mind, in a moment reminiscent of the ending of *Psycho*.

You might be wondering how such a rich episode can be squeezed into just 50 minutes of screen time. Terrance Dicks grounds the Eagle fleet, so this is one of the rare episodes with little or no visual effects. As a result of this eschewing of model effects shows, the characters and dialogue get all the episode running time to themselves.

All in all, it's a very special episode for these reasons and more and one of the very best in year two.

MAYA'S COMPUTER

ANALYSIS

10/10

Uncle Terrance, as he was known to *Doctor Who* fans, delivers the goods and then some with a rich and potent script. A true gem with a standout performance from Landau, showing us his vulnerable side in a way which was uncommon for leading men of the period. There are no Eagles, and the spiral effect is poor by the standards of the series, but these things are mere quibbles. This is a superb episode, not to be missed.

THE SEANCE SPECTRE

With a title like 'The Séance Spectre', one could be forgiven for expecting an episode akin to season one's 'The Troubled Spirit', but sadly this is not the case.

However, the episode is another very solid outing from the writer of 'Journey to Where'.

Directed with real flare and loads of energy, the episode features some dynamic camera angles, too.

Sanderson, played by Ken Hutchinson, one of the actors who terrorised Dustin Hoffman in Sam Peckinpah's movie *Straw Dogs*, is not a rampaging monster played by a stunt man in a rubber suit, but a human crew member of Moon Base Alpha whose tough job and long stretches of duty have started to affect his mind, making him increasingly paranoid, obsessive and resentful toward what he sees as the dictatorship of Commander Koenig.

Despite a focus of action, this is nonetheless a far more grown-up plot idea than many of the notions from earlier in the season.

Sanderson needs psychological help and without it becomes a danger to himself and others.

There's fights and action aplenty in this episode, too.

Carolyn Seymour from *The Survivors* series by Terry Nation also appears in the episode. One of the writers on *The Survivors*, Jack Ronder, wrote 'Brian the Brain' earlier in the season.

Seymour is typically superb in her role, bringing her striking screen presence to the episode.

We get a gripping and spectacular sequence where Koenig and Maya are stranded after an Eagle crash and the crippled ship has to be brought back by remote control, losing part of itself as it breaks free from an alien planet.

Best of all, the finale of the episode is really well done.

Sanderson and Koenig must fight on the Moon's surface as Koenig races against time to detonate more nuclear waste in order to redirect the Moon away from collision with Tora.

The episode continues the upward spike in quality and maturity of storytelling of the last eight episodes and is another reason the later episodes should perhaps have been screened earlier, to get the audience more engaged with the show.

MAYA'S COMPUTER

ANALYSIS

8/10

This is a pretty strong episode with lots of action and suspense and a memorable guest cast. The script is very well done and there is a feeling the season has now hit its stride, regularly reaching high levels of entertainment. The direction is dynamic and there are some great effects moments, too.

DORZAC

Dorzac (Lee Montague) is a criminal on board an alien ship which lands on Alpha. But he comes from Psychon and Maya knows him and believes him to be a good man. Alan Carter, meanwhile, finds himself romantically drawn to the woman who captains the alien ship. Is Dorzac friend or foe?

In an interview on the topic of producing *Space: 1999*, Sylvia Anderson, the producer of year one and co-creator of the series, talked at length about her wish to give Nick Tate more to do on screen and how this led to early creative clashes with Martin Landau.

She felt Tate was an interesting young actor with a good presence on screen but explained that when she attempted to get more interesting scenes for the Alan Carter character, such as Alan being temporarily in command of Alpha in Koenig's absence, there was a protest from Martin Landau that "Nick Tate is saying my lines."

Scripts were accordingly changed and re-written to let Koenig give all the orders.

So, it is interesting to note that with Fred Freiberger doing double up episodes in order to speed up the shooting schedule on season two, there are a number of episodes in which Koenig's part is greatly reduced and Alan Carter does, in fact, get to do a lot more than just fly Eagles.

In 'Space Warp', for example, Koenig is away in space with Tony and so Alan is left in charge of the base and is seen giving orders, making decisions and taking charge of the hunt for the runaway Maya.

In 'The Beta Cloud', with Koenig and Helena bed ridden, Alan is seen talking back-and-forth via video calls to Tony and Maya as they battle with cloud creature and to Bill Fraser whom he hands over to Sandra for instructions on how to make the cable barrier.

In the 'Mark of Archanon', Alan also has a major role as he befriends alien boy Etrec and bonds with him through the game of football.

But it is with this episode, 'Dorzac' that we have no Landau or Bain at all because they were away on a vacation during the shoot.

Here, Alan gets to be the romantic lead, something which probably should have been in a number of previous episodes, too, given his popularity.

He has a memorable romance with alien woman Sahala, a romance which is made complicated by her role as the Captain of a prison ship containing a dangerous criminal.

These episodes which focus heavily on the character of Alan Carter give us a chance to see one of Sylvia Anderson's ideas finally realised, albeit not under her reign as producer, and also give us an idea of what the series might have been like had Landau and Bain left the show and Alan Carter had taken control as the new Commander of the Moon Base.

The plot here is another example of why the last eight episodes of *Space: 1999* represent a step up from the first half of season two. Instead of the usual monsters, we have a scheming, manipulative humanoid alien who has the ability to turn good people to serve his evil purposes like some sort of alien version of Charles Manson, a charismatic leader whose cult will do his bidding, even when it is evil.

It is also another episode which focuses on the idea that having alien Maya as a regular on the base may well be a dangerous liability at times, in the Alphans' struggle for survival.

Dorzac is a member of Maya's own people, the Psychons. As with 'Space Warp' and 'The Dorcons', the presence of Maya on the base brings serious trouble. She firmly believes the prisoner in the visiting alien ship, the titular Dorzac, is a good man and convinces the Alphans to treat the visiting aliens with suspicion.

With Tony, Alan and Maya unsure about who can be trusted for most of the episode, this ends up being a compelling, intriguing and intelligent story and remains one of the most popular episodes of *Space: 1999*'s second season.

MAYA'S COMPUTER

ANALYSIS

9/10

Another little gem with some great material for the supporting cast while the stars are away. Maya has a very interesting role and Alan Carter gets to be the romantic lead his fans no doubt wanted to see.

DEVIL'S PLANET

Koenig finds himself alone on a prison planet ruled by a ruthless woman and her team of whip wielding women in red who like to hunt people for sport.

It's great to see Roy Marsden, a couple of years before his brilliant lead role in The Sandbaggers, playing Crael in this episode. (We couldn't see him in 'Rules of Luton'. He was invisible!) He and the two main women are really good performers who elevate this episode with their talents. This is a cracking, or perhaps whip-cracking, episode, with plenty of pace and action and a nice chance to see Koenig as the main focus of the story.

Roy Marsden is not given the most meaty or complex role in the story. Nevertheless, there are moments we see flashes of the inner steel later seen in his work playing such characters as the head of *The Sandbaggers* and the famous Detective *Inspector Dalgliesh*.

George Orwell's novel *Nineteen Eighty-Four* is referenced overtly in the episode, when Koenig mentions the concept of Double Think.

This positions the story firmly as one of dictatorship and the abuse of power. The character of Elizia, played with power by Brian Blessed's wife Hildegarde Neil, conceals an unpleasant truth from her people that they are the only survivors of their people, due to a deadly plague on their home planet. When Koenig is locked up in a prison cell with some of the prisoners, he tries to tell them the truth he has stumbled upon, but just as he is beginning to convince his fellow prisoners that he might be telling the truth, he is drowned out by a broadcast of what we would now call Fake News.

This idea of the media as a stooge for the ones in power, broadcasting misleading and manufactured information, still seems relevant today. But of course, this is also an adventure series so it's not all politics and power games. Nevertheless, this is far more intellectually interesting stuff than popcorn episodes like 'Space Warp', for example.

So, there is plenty of fun to be had with this episode. The first ten minutes are particularly strong. There is a spectacular crash landing of an Eagle in the woods on the penal planet. Koenig's fellow traveller Blake is annihilated by a disintegrating force barrier shortly after the pair stumble upon an event known as the hunt, on this planet. It's rather like one of those reality shows where the contestant is put through some rigorous task and the prize in this case is a trip back home to the mother planet.

The hunters are all female and dressed in red and they are armed with whips. Inevitably the Commander is going to become the quarry in the hunt in this outer space version of Survivor, in the episode's finale. Of course, the Commander is a cunning and clever man who does very well in the hunt and cleverly turns the tables by backtracking to the starting point to confront the Mistress of the penal colony.

The ending of the episode is very well done with the Commander turning everyone against his opponent by exposing her lies and deception so that they will turn against her and force her to travel back to the mother planet in pursuit of the Commander. She tries to kill him but the lethal pathogen on the mother planet strikes her down very fast.

It seems a fitting ending for such a tyrant and the episode serves as a good early taste of the type of politically charged Orwellian science fiction which would become enormously popular on British television just a couple of years later in *Blake's 7.*

One of the interesting points in the episode is that the writer seems to make a very clear point of defining the leadership style of the Commander Koenig character. I can only assume this was done deliberately because the whole episode is focused on the manipulative and totalitarian leadership style of Elizia.

By stark contrast to her leadership style, the Commander is defined as a leader who is willing to listen to the opinions of those under his command and consider their differing points of view before making decisions. It is also pointed out that he yields to their wishes occasionally, when he thinks it is right.

This is presumably why the Commander is a far better and more successful leader to his people than Elizia is to hers. The Commander is portrayed as almost egalitarian, which would make Alpha a classless society in which equality is its greatest social strength.

The main guest stars are excellent and although Koenig is the only one of the lead actors to appear in the episode there is a good role for the character of Bill Fraser, and this is one of the episodes which features Dr Ed Spencer and Alibe.

These are two newcomers who are excellent supporting characters who deserved more screen time and are played by very good actors we would have benefitted from seeing more of in the series.

All in all, this is another solid contribution to the final third of the series and continues the enormous upswing in quality of writing and production.

MAYA'S COMPUTER

ANALYSIS

7/10

This is a pretty decent episode with a great villainess and a nice theme. The costumes for the women who whip their quarries are vivid and memorable and the hunt is suspenseful enough. And it is great to see Roy Marsden bring his considerable screen presence to the series.

IMMUNITY SYNDROME

On an Earth like planet, an unknown life force exists which seeks to make contact but can kill without knowing it.

The force turns the entire planet hostile to a visiting Alpha party, sending Tony out of his mind. Koenig must find a way to make contact with the mysterious life force.

Despite the title which was borrowed from Trek by Fred Freiberger, this is a Johnny Byrne story about an immortal, shapeless being of light and energy who is unaware that other intelligent life exists and brings down death upon them until communication and understanding is accomplished.

The late Tony Anholt gives his best acting performance in the entire series in this episode. When he looks at the immortal alien creature and is blinded by the dazzling light of its undulating form, he is driven out of his mind.

Tony goes berserk, running across the surface of the planet and Koenig has to chase him down. It is an absolutely superb performance by Anholt and he displays great vulnerability when he has to explain what he saw and experienced.

The special effects department delivers some fabulous visuals for this episode. When an Eagle breaks up in flight, catches fire on the inside and eventually ploughs into the woods and explodes, it is a truly spectacular sequence from Brian Johnson and his team. Equally as good is a sequence in which Helena and Maya travel down to the planet in a futuristic glider which passes through a spectacular storm before making a forced landing on the surface of the planet.

And Bill Fraser comes across as such a cool and awesome character in his brief moments on screen that I can only conclude we really needed to see more of him in the show.

The main guest actor Nadim Swahalha is the father of actress Julia who became famous for the TV series *Press Gang* and *Absolutely Fabulous*. He does a great job as the dying alien in the hologram recordings the humans find, a very far cry from the Grasshopper of 'Space Warp'.

The ending of the episode is truly exhilarating and mind-expanding television as the heroic Koenig confronts the alien "I, that am I" and shows him trust, leading to communication, contact and understanding.

Easily in my top five fave episodes of the second season, this is an intelligent and memorable episode with plenty of action, suspense and drama to recommend it.

Even the most hard-bitten year one fan would find something to enjoy here, and it is not surprising that it is a script from *Space:1999*'s most prolific script writer.

MAYA'S COMPUTER

ANALYSIS

10/10

An absolute gem and a reminder of why this is such a great series. Exciting set pieces, chases, Eagle crashes and other model effect sequences, and plenty of peril keep the audience gripped and the final revelation of the alien life form is superb science fiction.

THE DORCONS

'The Dorcons' is a fantastic episode of *Space: 1999*. It is also written by the same writer who wrote 'The Metamorph'. It seems ridiculous to think that this and 'Immunity Syndrome' were pushed to the very end of the season, as if Johnny Byrne was not the show's most prolific contributor but a naughty child made to sit down the back corner of the classroom, out of better people's way.

Like most of Johnny Byrne's scripts for the series, they are first rate in all the ways that really count, so they really should have been shown early in the season, with 'The Metamorph'.

At least if 'The Dorcons' had been shown immediately after 'The Metamorph', we would have had an episode which focused completely on the character of Maya, immediately following her introduction. In view of the time it takes to write a TV script, it probably was produced last because that was when the script was ready, but 'The Dorcons' does appear to be a script in which Johnny Byrne, having introduced this super hero alien, this female Spock, considers what might come of having an alien living on Alpha as a permanent addition to the crew and, importantly, the consequences of that change to the Alpha situation. Byrne's assumption seems to be that Maya could turn out to be as much trouble as she's worth, bringing down the wrath of aliens whom the hapless humans have little chance of standing up to.

This is a really good reason the episode would have worked well as episode two of year two because it immediately raises the question: is she more of a liability that an asset to Alpha? Even if, as an audience, we eventually conclude Maya is an asset on the whole and great to have around, the fact it adds complexity to the situation very early on would be a good thing. Complexity means it's still a show for grown-ups, a show where things aren't black and white, and Maya is not just a comic book character, despite her origin story's close resemblance to that of *Superman* or the way she was promoted in the US as 'the *Wonder Woman* of Science Fiction'.

In the episode, her presence is what brings down the wrath of the Dorcons upon the Alphans, giving them a serious case of Buyer's Remorse. In fact, in one scene, Dorcon spokeswoman Varda asks if the Alphans are all willing to die for their principles. This leads to a terrific moment where one Alphan suggests giving Maya to them and another actually pulls a laser and has to be overpowered.

And in the midst of the base being attacked and this sort of mutinous, anti-Maya drama breaking out, actress Catherine Schell gets to deliver possibly her best moment of acting in all of *Space:1999* when Helena takes the man's laser gun. Maya, aware that she's facing a fate worse than death and appalled by what she's brought upon the Alphans, actually begs Helena to kill her. It's a brilliant moment, incredibly tense and well played by all. Helena even looks like she's seriously considering pulling the trigger for a few moments, too, until Koenig shouts loud enough to snap her out of it. It's a brilliant scene and tells us Maya is worth having on the show.

Another good reason for 'The Metamorph' to have been followed by this episode is that fans of *Space: 1999* were probably hoping for more of the same kind of thing they enjoyed in season one and this episode does deliver some of the goods. As with the season one classic the 'War Games', this episode features many sections of Moon Base Alpha being hammered and blasted into smouldering, twisted, metal pieces by a savage and merciless alien attack. There are plenty of spectacular explosions and good old Aussie hero and chief pilot Alan takes the Eagle fleet up to fight back.

We see an Eagle explode in a ball of fire and the underground Command Center of Moon base Alpha is revealed to be far from impervious as it is seriously damaged in the attack, panels belching smoke, girders crashing down, stunt men getting buried in debris and hurled across the room.

In fact, this is the only time in season two aliens really land some serious damage on the Alphans from space. If nothing else, it might have served to demonstrate that this was still, at least to some degree, the same spectacular series which had given us the opening 15 minutes of 'War Games', in which

Alpha was all but pulverised by aliens and their Hawk fighter ships. Okay, this is not in the same league as 'War Games'. It's not even in the same galaxy. But the Dorcon ship looks cool and the combination of model shots, miniature explosions, stunts, explosive set pieces and human drama with Alphans turning against Maya and Koenig battling to stay in control is really well edited together and generates some palpable excitement.

Former *Doctor Who* Patrick Troughton appears as the Dorcon ruler while actor Gerry Sundquist is very good as the scheming Malik. Sadly, in real life, the actor committed suicide, a few years after his appearance on the series. Ann Firbank is very good indeed as the charming and icy yet ultimately fair-minded Consul Varda.

MAYA'S COMPUTER

ANALYSIS

9/10

A genuinely exciting final episode where the Alphans are ready to die for Maya, the wonderful, heroic, and super powered alien woman who has saved them many times this season. Great guest stars, topped off by former *Doctor Who* Patrick Troughton, and an array of exciting model work and pyrotechnics enliven a strong, conflict filled dramatic script. It may not wrap up the season in any definitive manner, but it leaves us wishing for a third season and further adventures for the people of Moon Base Alpha.

MESSAGE FROM MOON BASE ALPHA

Although this is a short video production not produced as part of the *Space: 1999* TV series, 'Message from Moon Base Alpha' is well worth watching if you are able to locate a copy of it.

Written by Johnny Byrne and starring Zienia Merton as Sandra this is a short production made 20 years after the original series ended.

The film shows a message transmitted from the wandering moon by Sandra and in it she tells us that the Alphans have abandoned the Moon Base to live on a new planet called Terra Alpha.

In a final twist it is revealed that the message when received on Earth in an encoded form is actually the Meta signal from 'Breakaway' which was being picked up on Earth.

The writing and acting in 'Message from Moon Base Alpha' is very good indeed. People have often criticised the series over the years and claimed that the characters were not particularly well developed or three-dimensional and many critics claimed the series lacked emotion or warmth.

I mention this because when I watched 'Message from Moon Base Alpha' for the first time I found it to be an extremely moving and emotional experience. In fact, I was reduced to tears by the experience. I found it extremely touching and evocative of my memories of the series and what it had meant to me over the years.

Unlike the secret bases of various organisations in other Anderson series Moon Base Alpha truly became a home to the people who found themselves living in it and the Alphans very much became a kind of TV family. Sandra asks that we do not forget the people of Moon Base Alpha.

I'm sure we will remember them forever. They will remain always in our hearts, we will be Alphans with them and we will travel on their space odyssey as fellow adventurers in our dreams and imagination.

MAYA'S COMPUTER

ANALYSIS

10/10

An incredibly moving and sweet little mini episode which reminds us why we love the series and the inhabitants of Moon Base Alpha. Johnny Byrne's script is on point, the emotional moments are poignant and Zenia Merton does incredibly well, delivering more dialog here than she had in two seasons of the series. It's a final gem and absolutely a must-see viewing experience for fans who love this most extraordinary science fiction series. Never forget Moon Base Alpha.

ABOUT THE AUTHOR

Born in 1966, Adrian Sherlock grew up in working class Corio, in the Australian city of Geelong. He dreamed of writing, acting and film making. He got his first break in 1986, doing local theatre work before finding an agent in 1988. After a brief career in minor work in film and television, Adrian shifted into local theatre and studied to become a writer and teacher.

In 1999 he produced and performed in an independent television series called Damon Dark, which screened on Community TV (Channel 31) in Melbourne.

YouTube brought him back to film making and acting in 2006 when he helped launch web series such as Damon Dark and Vincent Kosmos.

In 2012, he performed a one-man stage show in Geelong, based on his Damon Dark UFO hunter character.

Adrian Sherlock is also a writer, whose first published novel was a tie-in to the Doctor Who television series, titled Lethbridge-Stewart: The New Unusual and published by Candy Jar Books.

He has a journalism degree and an MA in writing and has written several viewer's guidebooks about classic British TV series which inspired him.

Printed in Great Britain
by Amazon

40091743R00185